BARANTINED

BARANTINED

RECIPES, TIPS, & STORIES TO ENJOY AT HOME

MIKE WOLF

TURNER
PUBLISHING COMPANY

Turner Publishing Company
Nashville, Tennessee

www.turnerpublishing.com

Barantined: Recipes, Tips, and Stories to Enjoy at Home

Cover design: Jess Machen
Book design: Stacy Wakefield Forte
Photos: Brooke Dainty

Library of Congress Control Number: 2021937144

9781684426928 Hardback
9781684426935 Ebook

Printed in the United States of America

"WON'T SOUL MUSIC CHANGE,
NOW THAT OUR SOULS HAVE
TURNED STRANGE?"

DAVID BERMAN

CONTENTS

DANDELION ALASKA *p. 131*

THE DRINKS

THE GREEN VACCINE

SPIEGELAUDER

THE CIVIL SERVICE

TRASHMOPOLITAN

NUMBER ONE

THIEF'S ALIBI

GOLDEN HOUR

APERITIF BELIEF

MAYA BAY

QUEEN OF THE RODEO

DRO'S TOM KAH

OTRO VEZ

AUTOMATIC SUPERSONIC HYPNOTIC FUNKY FRESH

"WHAT DAY IS IT?"

LITTLE MARIE

THE ONLY WAY TO SAY FAREWELL

SHELTER COVE

CHAMOMILE COOLER

FRAPPÉ-STYLE DAIQUIRI

SPRUCE TIP GIMLET

TEMPEST OF TANSY

CATAVINO

PEAS EXCUSE ME

SAKE AND SPICE

YELLOW EYES

BOOZY BANANA BREAD

EPISODE 2: THE BREAKFAST FIZZ

MUTUALLY ASSURED

DESTRUCTION

HAPPENSTANCE

THE GOOD SAMARITAN

GOOD AS GOLD

MR. SPARKLE

THE BOLD ADVENTURE

TERRA FIRMA MIX

PANIC BUTTON

WISCONSIN APPLE PIE

COME OUT TONIGHT

ADRIANA

SAFE WORD

COMING UP ROSES

THE SPAGHETTI WESTERN

CLASSIC SPANISH VERMOUTH COCKTAIL

HOT TADASHI

DIAMOND CUTTER

STANDARD PROOF WILDFLOWER LEMONADE

FOXY BROWN

THAT'S A PEACH HUN

WE GOT THE JAZZ

ZICATELA

MEADMOSA

BOXED-IN SOUR

CHARLIE'S OLD FASHIONED #3

OH HAI!

ENDLESS SUMMER OLD-FASHIONED

Whiskey and records can help pass the time.

As someone who loves restaurants and bars—working in *and* frequenting them— it has been hard to watch the industry endure so much upheaval over the past year and a half. Working on this book and gathering stories, thoughts, and recipes from hospitality professionals going through a global pandemic only made me miss it more. →

Part of what I love about hospitality is how people give so much of themselves to provide an unforgettable experience for someone else. In a way, it binds us together. Sometimes it can be as simple as making someone feel welcome; opening up in a way that makes the guest feel like they belong. Other times, it involves empathizing with total strangers and guiding them through a meal, maybe even broadening their horizons when it comes to food and drink. So much of it is just doing whatever you can to brighten someone else's day. I found this same level of hospitality in many of the contributors' responses, and I can't thank them enough for sharing their honest feelings about what they were going through. While some were contemplating new careers and different places to live, I was emailing them to open up and share during a very difficult time. Looking back, I think about all the emails I sent to my colleagues badgering them for responses, and I remember a fleeting sense of community. I felt closer to them, but somehow disconnected at the same time. When I began to read through what they wrote, I was touched as I realized we were all going through the same thing in different ways. It felt *intense* to correspond about the real challenges we were all up against. Selfishly, that's probably what led me to keep pushing and get it done. I enjoyed engaging with these people I admired and respected and hoped we could at least raise some money for a good cause and create a time capsule from a period we wouldn't ever forget.

The idea for this project came from discussions with Stephanie Bowman at Turner Publishing, who helped guide this book along the way. I had been working on a new book all about the second "golden age of the cocktail in America," how all over the country and the world, people were drinking better than they ever had. Cocktail dens in places as far-flung as Tucson, Tulsa, Lafayette, and Lincoln were combining mastery of the classics with bold experimentation to forge a delicious new era of drinking. It had never been easier to find a good Negroni. I wanted to explore this idea further, which I had turned into a podcast with my buddy Kenneth Dedmon, as well as check in on the exciting worlds of cider, spirits, wine, beer, and anything else I could put in my glass. After opening Chopper, a tropical drinks miasma of robots and fire, and releasing *Garden to Glass: Grow Your Drinks from the Ground Up,* a summation of the trials and errors of gardening and creating drinks from nature's bounty, I was thirsty for new experiences beyond what I'd been working on for the previous seven years. I called Stephanie in May of 2020 to say, "I can't really write what I thought I'd be able to. It doesn't make sense anymore," admitting defeat and wondering if every other writer was calling to tell her the same. They were, except for the ones who had old pandemic theories to expand into books on the fly.

It's great talking to Stephanie because she doesn't bullshit, and she knows if I'm dancing around an idea that might be decent. She asked, "What's going on with all your friends who bartend and work in the service industry?" I took a deep breath and thought through the dozens of things I'd heard over the phone, from staying open and risking too much, to closing and moving closer to family only to experience *more* strife. I was overcome with emotion for a second and just let out a "Whoaaaaaa, that's a heck of a question."

"Maybe there's a book there," she said. "We can try to raise some money for people who are struggling right now."

The idea of doing something of-the-moment during a global pandemic was inspiring and daunting. We decided I would get a few months to cull together as much material as I could, bartenders would submit recipes of some of their favorite creations, and we'd put it out as an eBook, with an expanded hardcover to follow. That eBook came out as *Lost Spring: How We Cocktailed Through Crisis* in late August 2020, benefitting Tennessee Action for Hospitality, an amazing nonprofit providing grants for hospitality workers in need in Tennessee. The expanded hardcover is the book you hold in your hands.

When I started this project, I made a list of all the incredibly talented hospitality folks I knew and created a questionnaire centered around the changing nature of our industry. The questions I asked were:

+ What have you missed most about the hospitality industry and the job you had before the pandemic?

+ What books, shows, or music have helped you through the Lost Spring?

+ Does this experience change your approach to bartending postpandemic?

+ What has been the hardest part about this for you?

+ What positive things happened to you during the Lost Spring?

I also asked any wine professionals for tips on buying wine on the cheap, and pairing wine with frozen foods. What I realized as the responses came pouring in was that I was extremely blessed to know all these people and count them as colleagues and friends.

When it came time to expand the eBook—something I cover more in-depth in the "Comfort Booze" chapter—I realized that while I had been spending the last few years of my career creating complex drinks, what I really craved were the bare-bones classics: Old-fashioned, Manhattan, Martini, Negroni, like a cocktail Mount Rushmore. So I wanted to include more of those classics and give recipes on the simplest—but most crucial—details inherent in mastering them. Then something else happened. With so much time to work in the garden, I became inspired. I began to miss the process of making complicated cordials and bitters from scratch and creating bold, unique cocktails, so I added a few of those in the book as well. Since I was at home with my two kids, Henry and Leila, who were both doing virtual school, I wasn't sharing my garden with restaurant and bar customers anymore. So, with all the botanicals I grew, harvested, and dried, I made a vermouth with the folks at Love and Exile Wines in Nashville. This shiso-forward, rosé dry vermouth is featured in the "Don't Forget About the Bamboo" cocktail on page 137. It was a fun project and something I'd always wanted to do.

When it came time to write the introduction for the eBook, it felt like the whole world was changing right before my eyes, because it was. It was the first week of June, 2020, and any sense of camaraderie that we developed through the initial lockdown phase in this country was going up in smoke, like the wildfires raging across the west. My mind was metamorphic, somber and searching for answers one moment, angry and frustrated the next. The backbone through it all were my wife and children, and I'll be forever grateful for the extra time spent with them. Now I'm sitting here writing this with a sore arm from getting my first shot of the vaccine. I can see hope in the distance, and rest a little easier knowing my parents and a few of my immunocompromised friends are completely vaccinated. I suppose the future is always uncertain, but I feel especially sympathetic for those who have had to completely change careers and forge a whole new path. Some of the contributors of this book won't be going back to work in restaurants and bars, and that's okay. I know there will be a day soon enough when I can welcome them into my home, my bar, or maybe just my home bar, and make them something that will brighten their day. I hope this book brightens yours.

FROM THE LOST SPRING TO BARANTINED

The place where I began bartending is also the place where I met my wife. It was called K's China, a Vietnamese and Chinese restaurant and bar in Boulder, Colorado. →

It was across the street from the University of Colorado campus and had good food, steady but strange bar business through the colder months, and bands of all genres playing shows on the weekends. There was even a "Reggae Night," hosted by some talented musicians from Jamaica who had a radio show in town and were permitted to smoke grass on the balcony for "religious reasons." In the summer, the small bar on the main level—with only five seats—became a monster, with up to two hundred people filing into the space and heading upstairs to the rooftop patio, which was only open during the warmer months. With its own bar and jaw-dropping views of the Flatirons and the front range of the Rocky Mountains stretching north to Estes Park, the patio called to a thirsty clientele with a penchant for drinking multiple Volcano Bowls in one sitting. The rooftop would be jam-packed on really busy nights and could—when things got wild—transform into what resembled a scene out of a Jean-Claude Van Damme movie: a nasty fight in one corner involving questionable martial arts and a tracksuit, while someone else took their clothes off and threatened to jump off the balcony on the other side of the bar. It wasn't always so crazy, though. There were also plenty of blissfully small moments, like when the sun was just begin-ning to set over the Flatirons on an early summer evening, The Velvet Underground's *Loaded* record was queued up on the rooftop sound system, the Jamaicans were smoking, and nobody, as the song goes, felt any pain. As I sat at home throughout quarantine in 2020, I would think back to memorable nights like these at crowded bars, both as a bartender and a patron.

I remember presiding over a rambling and alcohol-fueled discussion one night between a psychology professor and a former student, regarding the "locus of control," and how it tended to change as one got older. The term fascinated me and has stuck in my head ever since that night. I even wrote a song about it years ago. The locus of control describes the degree to which people feel like they have control over the events that shape their lives. There are only two sides to this coin: those who believe they have control over their own lives, and those who feel as though their lives are controlled by outside forces, such as fate or chance. Like many people in 2020, I felt my grip on whatever control I thought I had over my life slowly slip away. I'm not a fatalist, and here was one of the first times when I really felt like outside forces were in charge, like a storm. Only this time, the uncomfortable calm came *after* the storm, as cities shut down around the world and bustling neighborhoods became eerily quiet. A harbinger of doom, a real-life nightmare, a time to be alone—whether you wanted to be or not. In an era when families were forced to choose between saying goodbye over a smartphone or not saying goodbye at all, complete with a devastating tornado *and* nearly every restaurant and bar shutting down at once, the spring of 2020 in Nashville, Tennessee, was shocking, tragic, and surreal.

I'm proud to write this from Nashville, where I saw so many amazing people banding together to deal with a historic natural disaster that happened *before* COVID-19 came to change life in America as we know it. Just as the virus was beginning to spread in parts of Washington state and New York City, an EF-3 tornado with winds of 165 mph ripped through the heart of Nashville, damaging or destroying upwards of 771 buildings and killing twenty-four people across four counties, including five children in nearby Putnam County, where the winds reached 175 mph. The only two people who died in the city of Nashville, in Davidson County, were rock-star, on-the-rise bartenders, Albree Sexton and Michael Dolfini, a loving couple who lived in East Nashville and worked at top-flight bars. Albree held court at the Fox Bar and Cocktail Club, while Michael mixed things up at the Nashville outpost of needs-no-introduction, Attaboy Lounge. Though I didn't know them well, their influence on this book and the contributors herein is immense (Riley Perrin, Laura Unterberg, and Adam Sloan both have compassionate, insightful thoughts on their passing). Comrades and guests alike spoke glowingly and affectionately of a couple who came to Nashville in search of a little more space and a laid-back vibe. They loved the people and the hospitality of the bar business and, like many of the bartenders in this book, were incalculably creative.

As we reached the one-month mark of quarantine, and answers still couldn't keep up with all the questions on our minds (what day is it, again?), and the unemployment hotlines succumbed to the weight of a world with no work to do, there were glimmers of hope in the darkness, like light piercing through a keyhole. "We're going to come together like we did during 9/11," we collectively thought for a few weeks. "We can do this if we drop the politics and agree on a strategy," we said for a few days in late April. Masks, the ones we've watched people in Asia and beyond wear for the last few decades as they've dealt with SARS and other outbreaks, suddenly became a fact of life in a re-emerging society. These masks became predictably politicized by pouty adults of all ages who crossed their arms, huffed in place like churlish little children (as a parent-in-chief during these times, I've come to know the attitude well), and demanded that things GET BACK TO NORMAL! Some, to my continual amazement, went so far as to protest by harassing the very doctors and nurses who were risking so much to manage the historical quagmire of COVID-19.

So much for coming together. It didn't really work out the way I expected. As I sit here writing this on the doorstep of an uncertain summer, the pandemic has been overlaid with racial justice protests, pulsing through the country amid a reckoning with the racism that has flowed undeterred in this country like rivers flowing in multiple directions from an ever-present Continental Divide that can't be dammed and won't be damned, no matter how many Black people are killed by cops.

We'll be wondering whether the killings of George Floyd, Ahmaud Arbery, Breonna Taylor, and Rayshard Brooks were the final straws that began to break the bonds of institutional racism, and what effect the shutdown had on—in these early stages—a real reckoning to set the stage for change. It might have been too much to ask of a perpetually divided society to come together as a whole for the greater good. Maybe a national crisis (or several) is what it took to make us all look hard in the mirror and realize that if we weren't part of the solution, we were diligently ignoring the problem. If you can't make it easier for disadvantaged people to vote and participate in a democracy, it's much more difficult to believe you live in one. If you make it harder for those who have less, it becomes easier to accept, because that's just the "way things are," and because confronting the core of racism in America is uncomfortable and reaches into the far recesses of history that none of us were taught in school. Both the Tulsa Race Massacre of 1921 and the Sand Creek Massacre of 1864 come to mind. We're in the middle of yet another transformative period in our history, but like the Sand Creek Massacre of Cheyenne and Arapaho Native Americans, which was apart from but intrinsically related to the Civil War, the reasons are both separate and deeply embedded, like roots of two different plants tangled together underground. We emerged out of the spring of 2020 more divided *because* we were kept apart, and because what sells in the media culture today is to staunchly trash the opposition and seek no middle ground. Without concerts to enjoy and long family dinners in a crowded restaurant where laughs can collide with different political ideals, the commonalities that helped bond us together—like sweet vermouth mingling with exotic bitters and aged whiskey to become a Manhattan—became lost in a sea of misinformation and, later, conspiracy theories that divided families. While a warm and cozy idea at first, then maddeningly out of reach a month later, we *are*, in fact, in this big ol' mess together. The struggles of this time and the past that informs it, like the warnings of the Spanish Flu of 1918, will provide us with decades of wisdom. What we'll do with it and where we'll end up is still being written, and that makes for some inspiring times. If only the times weren't so damn sad.

One afternoon in late March, near the beginning of quarantine, I broke an eight-day homebound stretch and took the longest route possible to get to my neighborhood bottle shop, driving some back roads, slowly traipsing my way through the east entrance to Shelby Park. My mind was heavy with so many things: a jumble of headlines, my friends losing jobs, the anxiety our family shared over the growing intensity of my wife Kate's shifts as an emergency room nurse at Vanderbilt University Health Center, cancelling all the trips for my book tour for *Garden to Glass*, how long it would be before I'd see my parents and my brother's family in Colorado, and how my kids were going to handle being shuttered in the house for weeks on end. But then, the sight of a house completely destroyed in the wake of the tornado hit me like a left hook to the jaw. My chest began to feel tight, my eyes a little blurry from the onions I wasn't cutting, and I suddenly realized the road to recovery for Nashville in the wake of one of the worst tornadoes the state had ever seen was just beginning and was now more tangled and complicated than the downed tree limbs still resting on ripped-open rooftops. Volunteers couldn't help to clear neighborhoods of debris or distribute supplies to their neighbors, nor could they find hope and comfort in the shared spirit of camaraderie that so many were able to feel as the city rebounded in those days after the tornado. I wanted to do something to help Nashville in the wake of what I was beginning to call the Lost Spring, and I hope the funds from this book can contribute to the cause.

The phrase Lost Spring, something we started throwing around on my podcast *Liquid Gold*, with native Nashvillian bartender and writer Kenneth Dedmon, was a reference to all the ideas and beautiful cocktails that, in the cold and leafless days of early March, were being fleshed out in bars all over the country, that would now be lost to time and circumstance. Would these creations make a comeback on summer menus down the road? What of the seasonality and vibrancy of those sours and cobblers? In the spring of 2021, will we get right back on the horse and dust these ideas off? Not so fast, it appears, and by the time spring of 2021 rolls around, beverage professionals will have more new ideas (some will even have new careers), filtered through all the time they spent pondering, reading, writing, and listening. Getting *inspired*. That's one thing about the time away from bartending for so many professionals: there was time to reinvest in our own well-being, be creative, slow down a little. One thing I heard from many of my colleagues was "there's not enough time in the day, I'm never bored, I'm trying to get everything done and I'm not doing anything. It's bizarre!" Okay, I added that last part. However, for those of us who have small children, it was more "God help me, I'm out of board games!" In the meantime, and I'm sure you could use a drink by now, I hope there is some solace to be found in hearing about how some of your favorite bartenders managed to make a few of their favorite drinks, along with some lovely, painful, honest, and wise words. There are plenty of music and binge-watching suggestions, and even some wine pairings for frozen food. How 2020 is that? I hope this can fill in somewhat for the conversations you might have had while posted up at a bar and drinking something special during a unique period in our history, which will always be (to me anyway) the Lost Spring, where so much was lost and, I still believe, much will be gained.

—MIKE WOLF, NASHVILLE, TENNESSEE - JUNE 5, 2020

CHAPTER ONE

WHAT WE'VE MISSED

I'll never forget my last night behind the stick before bars and restaurants were effectively shut down all over the city to halt the spread of COVID-19. →

The entire evening played out like a good Hitchcock thriller, with an unnerving thread of risk running through every interaction. It was a night that had plenty to offer: old friends stopping by for a drink and catching up, neighborhood regulars showing off a perennial favorite to their parents from New York City, and other bartenders coming by to drink on an off night and talk shop. Then a customer began to feel ill and asked for the check suddenly, before the entrees were brought out, as customers at the bar began to squirm and move over a few seats, culminating in a Lysol raid and a slight panic. I inquired with a regular, "Oh, Marcus, how is your salad over there? Enjoying it?" He shot me a penetrating stare and a slow nod. Uh . . . yeah, times were definitely a-changing. Something was clearly amiss. It was as if you could feel the anxiety in the air, like humidity that sticks to your suit at a summer wedding in the South. But no one really *wanted* to believe that life was about to change. That's what I'll remember most about that night. Denial, embraced by a distressing segment of the country and encouraged by President Trump, was about to become part of the new normal.

As COVID-19 raged on throughout 2020, and I was relegated to stay-at-home-dad mode, I began to miss the people and the choreographed madness that can go into a night behind the bar. I missed the connection with both regulars and complete strangers where the intersection of music, sports, politics, binge-worthy television, and the world of food and drink are all fair game in the span of a few hours. I missed watching people become closer right there in front of me, sharing an intimacy that, oddly enough, wasn't possible in their own dining room. I missed the revelations shared with a guest over the perfect Pisco Sour, the well-balanced Mai Tai, or the Zombie that turns out to be everything they dreamed it would be. Most of all, I missed the camaraderie of a close staff, all working toward the same goal, to get through it all with dignity and make memories for guests, providing something we won't soon take for granted: the simple joy of a drink and a bite surrounded by friends, neighbors, and total strangers. What follows are more thoughts about what we all missed about bartending and hospitality while stuck at home quarantining.

My coworkers. I miss getting excited because there is an amazing staff working tonight.

—EDDIE ADAMS

We switched to takeout service during quarantine, and my husband, Hrant, and I could not figure out why it felt so off until we realized we missed the energy of the people. The buzz of the dining room on the weekend, all the friendly faces, hearing stories of adventure, and all the gracious compliments on their way out. It is easy to get caught up in the everyday drum of owning a business. You lose sight of why you are doing it in the first place.

—LIZ ENDICOTT :: LYRA

I definitely miss simply "bellying up" to local bars. I miss talking to local bartenders to see all the creative ways they are using whiskey.

—ROBERT LONGHURST :: STANDARD PROOF

The camaraderie. There is something so satisfying about being in the weeds and working as a team to pull it all off, and then sitting down for an end-of-the-night drink to go over the night. Also, I miss the ability to see all my friends and regulars night after night. It makes you feel connected with everyone, even if you're just pouring them a glass and watching their evening unfold.

—BRICE HOFFMAN :: WOODLAND WINE

Being in the flow of a pro staff is a wonderful experience, and I want to get back to that.

—GRAHAM FUZE :: BUTCHERTOWN HALL

The community, and seeing all of the great people enjoying spring in Nashville. My bar friends, customers, reps, coworkers . . .

—CRAIG SCHOEN :: PENINSULA

I have missed other people's energy most. Having so much time in solitude makes me appreciate how much we all affect one another. Humans are incredibly interesting.

—ALEXIS SOLER :: OLD GLORY, FALCON, CAMP, FLAMINGO

I miss being able to make people happy on a nightly basis, spending the time working toward a unified goal with the respective staffs. I miss riding the wave of a busy rush and seeing everyone work through their respective challenges in their station/section, coming out the other side, high fives and laughs wrapping up a night. General camaraderie as a whole—it's tough to be apart from people you normally spend ten- to twelve-hour shifts with several times a week.

—BRANDON BRAMHALL :: ATTABOY

For me, working in restaurants has always been about personal connections. Whether through our guests, employees, or purveyors, I miss the people I got to spend time with on a daily basis.

—ANDY WEDGE :: MOMOFUKU BAR WAYO, NYC

I'm in a unique position with this quarantine: I never stopped working, but my entire day-to-day was turned upside down. I work within a hotel, and with no real food and beverage outlets running, my day-to-day was switched to focus on a front desk position to help cover the lack of staff. So first and foremost, I miss the routine I had in place for the last year and a half. I'm not behind the stick much anymore, but those daily interactions with guests from all over the country and world were something I looked forward to, and it kills me it's not happening now. I live alone, so just the lack of human interaction has been hard. You would think working a welcome desk would help with the loneliness, but when you do not have guests in house, it does not make a difference.

—JOSHUA "WOODY" WILLIS :: 4TH AND PEABODY, NASHVILLE

The hospitality industry has been the identity of work as I know it since I was legally able to get my first job. From Savannah to New York to my current home in Charleston, I have only ever paid my bills in their entirety with cash flow generated within the walls of restaurants. Sure, my heart has shopped around for alternatives—for a way out, for some ambiguous and sparkling new career—but time after time I have chosen to stay put. A large part of the reason why is that I have never felt quite confident enough to monetize my passions, until . . . now. I was laid off in early March. While fear was certainly my first reaction, inspired action was a close second. I started to utilize my skills for the sake of simply sharing tools I knew to be useful. I sent an email to an old mailing list of mine offering quarts of homemade bone broth. Three months later and I have sold close to four hundred quarts of broth from my home kitchen (shhh!). I'm now left questioning whether this endeavor has marked the end of a very long chapter. Will I ever return to restaurant work as I knew it? I have missed all of the strange, dramatic drudgery of the day-to-day

life working in a restaurant. I miss the conversations, the bicker-
ing, the hustle, the generosity, the flavor, the camaraderie, and
the absurdity of it all.

—VILDA GONZALEZ :: MCCRADY'S, CHARLESTON

I miss the energy that only the hospitality industry can give.
This is an industry built on making sure others feel comfortable
and loved. As an owner of an events and catering company
(Hospitality 201), I miss the energy of events and seeing all of
my friends in the same place, celebrating and dancing together.
I miss sitting across from my friends at their bars and seeing
their creativity shine through a cocktail.

—CARLEY GASKIN :: HOSPITALITY 201, CHICAGO

I miss the friendships and camaraderie with my team. I miss the
jokes and seeing my favorite faces. I miss the excitement of the
night and rhythm of it all. I miss connecting over a cocktail and
bonding over shared experiences. Mostly, though, I miss the
nachos.

—JEREMIAH BLAKE :: BASTION LITTLE BAR, NASHVILLE

I miss the bartenders and servers that I get to work closely
with. They turn me on to all sorts of new music, books, shows,
games, etc. They help keep me young.

—MATT TOCCO :: STRATEGIC HOSPITALITY, NASHVILLE

I miss the silent language of sitting at a bar, the bartender
knowing exactly what you want before you even open your
mouth. The beautiful dance of serving people and being served,

I miss that the most. The wine conversations. For example, I start talking about Louis de Grenelle Saumur Sparkling Rosé and somehow within seconds we find out that the family living next door to my grandmother in Maine are the guests I'm speaking to at the table. The great reveal! The guest says, "I hate chardonnay," and I pour a taste of Roland Lavantureux Chablis. The guest says, "This is amazing, what is this wine?"

"It's chardonnay from France."

"Well then . . . I'll take two glasses."

—NICOLETTE ANCTIL :: SOMMELIER, HUSK, NASHVILLE

Connection, stability, money. All of these things will inevitably change forever. My favorite part of bartending has always been connecting with guests in a way that brings unexpected discovery and enlightenment—for them and for me. Many great friendships and collaborations that I've developed with people began with chance encounters; some have since told me stories of when they first met me as bar guests—how memorable it was and how it shifted their perspective or elevated their experience. I believe if I can cultivate a supper club–type outlet to share meals and drinks and love with people, the intimate connection and unique experience will thrive, but spontaneous interactions will be much fewer and further between.

Stability and money will be tough for our industry moving forward; one of the benefits of restaurant work has always been that it's not for everyone, but that if you can handle the hard work and social intricacies and showcase your talent, it will be lucrative and consistent. I don't know how long—if ever—it will be before consistency and profitability return to our industry.

—JESSICA BACKHUS :: HEAD BARTENDER, DELANEY OYSTER HOUSE, CHARLESTON

I miss all of the connections. Chatting with guests and sharing laughs with my coworkers is definitely my favorite part of working in this industry.

—NICK THAXTON :: CHOPPER

What I miss most about the hospitality industry are my coworkers, first and foremost, the *good* regulars (we all know the ones we treasure like gold), and the rush of a Friday or Saturday night when everyone and everything is moving like clockwork. That vibe, I miss the vibe. Where you can eye your "bartner" from across the bar and they already know what you need with just one look (I'm talking to you, T-Bone and Cass). The prediction of their next step, something you learn after many six- to eight-hour shifts together, so you know exactly where you're supposed to be or where you are *not* supposed to be (telling coworkers *"Behind!"* is still so underused). Your dance behind the bar—it should flow like the drinks you're pouring.

—ALICIA SWARTZ :: NASHVILLE

The food and beverage community is unlike anything in the world, so it's hard to pick just one thing I miss the most. As bars are unable to operate naturally, the world is completely void of one of its most beautiful communities that typically provides a second home or an essential escape. If I had one draft pick, I'd probably say that the thing I miss the most is the family vibe that you develop as a team behind the bar. There is no substitution for the feeling of cranking out hundreds of beautiful drinks on a busy night with a true and sacred homie. I never quite understood why the experience is so bonding so quickly, but it creates a level of hang that cannot be unlocked any other way. There's a special planet of comedy to explore, and together you're constantly discovering tasty treats and new flavor pairings. It's hard to imagine a more insane way to combine learning and friendship.

—PAUL ROGERS :: HEAD BARTENDER, MARSH HOUSE, NASHVILLE

I have missed hugs from friends. I have missed delicious meals and snacks that I don't have to prep or cook. I have missed the camaraderie that is the Nashville service industry. I have missed the brilliant minds that create wonderful cocktails with my brands. . . . It's kind of boring to do it alone.

—ERIN BARNETT :: SPIRIT ANIMAL CO OPERATIVE, NASHVILLE

I would have to say that I miss my team and regulars the most. It's not out of reach to say that those people who sustain you through each day and light up your work are a lot like family.

—MERCEDES O'BRIEN :: BAR MANAGER, COLD BEER, ATLANTA

I think the things I've missed the most about my work before the quarantine are the things that used to annoy me, and I took them for granted. I truly miss someone asking me to make their drink "strong" or berating me for not putting enough dirt in their dirty martinis. It at least meant they were engaging! Bring on the annoyance! I also really miss the camaraderie of a restaurant and the fun, quick conversations you have at the service well with the waitstaff, just shit-talking or checking in on how the night is going on the floor.

—TRAVIS ARCHER :: OSTERIA LA BUCA, LOS ANGELES

I've really missed my coworkers, honestly. The inside jokes, the ways you try make each other laugh during a shitty shift. Being quarantined with one person (my boyfriend of seven years) instead of a group you are used to working five to six shifts a week with is definitely a different dynamic. Maybe it's because we know each other too well at home, and my jokes really slap at work.

–KYNSEY HUNTER :: GREEN PHEASANT, NASHVILLE

I miss going to bars—alone or with my friends. Being surrounded by people, most of whom you never actually knew, but you were all there for the same reason: to drink, to be out of your house, to unwind, to decompress, to enjoy your friends' company. I miss serving people. I miss seeing my regulars, and making them their favorite cocktails. I miss meeting people from all over the world every day of the week. I miss hearing stories daily of other people's lives, struggles, and love. But most of all, I miss my friends. I miss Mike's laugh and Albree's hugs. And I miss my team. I miss being in our little bar, night after night, with the lights low and the candles lit behind us. I miss us all getting off work at 3:00 in the morning and sitting down with a cold Coors and being able to talk about anything and everything for hours into the morning. I miss Attaboy.

—RILEY PERRIN ELLIS :: ATTABOY, NASHVILLE

There are so many things I have missed, but I think the biggest one is my coworkers and guests. As a hospitality enthusiast, I miss being able to make someone's day better by simply making sure that the meal, drink, or experience is one so awesome they can—if just for an hour or two—forget about the woes of the day. I was and still am so looking forward to working with a new crew at the rooftop of the Graduate hotel.

—TARYN BREEN :: WHITE LIMOZEEN,
NASHVILLE AND JOSEPHINE, NASHVILLE

I would have to say that what I miss the most about the industry is the ability to play around with spirits and create new cocktails. I don't think most people realize how expensive it is to keep a well-stocked home bar, at least when it comes to making cocktails. In that same vein, I've been lucky enough to create cocktails for different events and dinners. Thanks to Arnold Myint, I've been fortunate enough to create cocktails for private events at the restaurant and the "Simmer" chef series put on by The Nashville Food Project, and, by far my proudest moment, two cocktails for Arnold's dinner at The James Beard House in New York City.

—MATT BURNETT :: PM, NASHVILLE

Sharing and relating with each guest has always been a priority, but what really stood out was bouncing these ideas off the people I worked with day in and day out. This is something I took for granted. When the time comes, I'll never do that again. This time has taught me to slow down and appreciate every little interaction with guests and coworkers. We never know when our last opportunity will present itself.

—ADAM MORGAN :: HEAD BARTENDER, HUSK, NASHVILLE

I miss the people! I miss hearing folks' stories, talking to strangers at the bowling alley. I'm on the supplier side now, but I spend one afternoon a week bartending at Avondale Bowl. Hospitality is the unique opportunity to make someone's day better, and it's just not as easy for me to turn that attention inward. I miss the catharsis of a three sink and a stack of glasses. I miss sharing new spirits with my bar friends and plotting cocktails. I miss traveling with my rum work and meeting enthusiasts around the country. I miss crowded tasting events, the breakdown and the shifties. I miss the feeling of a quiet hotel room as a respite from a hard day in a new city. Now every day is quiet.

—ADRIENNE STONER :: CHICAGO

I miss the stories my guests would tell me. That was my favorite part of the job, to start someone off on a tale and let the evening revolve around that, to let the bar be a place where stories are told. I wanted the patrons to think of themselves as audience and as tellers of stories, whether they be funny, sad, instructive, or wise. And I miss my favorite regulars, who knew they were my favorites because they could always be counted upon for a good tale. My favorite thing to do was create the conditions where someone could take center stage, and help that person enchant the other guests with memories of Australia and the Arctic, or stories of New York City cops and Jersey mafia, or tall tales of the hallowed halls of big DC firms and cool Memphis clubs, or memories of the Kentucky hills, good bourbon, and horse races, or inside information about the craziness of the music business, high society, and the rich history of Nashville, Tennessee.

I guess I have a big appetite for stories. And for hearing people speak from their experiences, especially older people, as many of my guests were. Maybe to replace that, I've been watching a lot of old movies, from the 1930s, '40s, '50s, '60s, '70s. If I were at the bar, I would ask my guests, "Do you remember anything like this happening before? How did you feel about it? How did you deal with it?" But I don't have the gift of their lived experiences, so I've been watching movies instead. How did people interpret trouble, plague, and war before this time? How did they imagine their response?

—LEAH SMITH :: ETCH, NASHVILLE

I've missed working with a team of people who are excellent at what they do, being able to make someone's day for a living, and making fourteen "vodka-sodas, splash cran" at once.

—SALLY GATZA :: BAR MANAGER, LA JACKSON, NASHVILLE

I miss interacting with people, the energy of the nightlife crowd, and sitting at a bar and shooting the shit with the bartender.

—ALI BESTEN :: CATHEAD, NASHVILLE

I miss getting to meet new people. I don't consider myself a social butterfly, but I loved getting to hear stories from guests at work. Working in a hotel was so fun to me because there is the possibility of meeting folks from all over the world and making friends that you otherwise would not have.

—DEMI NATOLI :: WHITE LIMOZEEN, NASHVILLE

The thing I miss the most is listening to people share stories at the bar. Whether sharing a funny anecdote with me, or maybe someone sharing something really sensitive, I miss hearing other people's experiences. I really missed this at Sunday Vinyl. There is something about loud music, good music, at the bar that brings people together. Music allows people to feel collective emotions, and I think experiencing all of that, plus great wine, plus great food, makes a restaurant a powerful experience.

—BRANDON ANAMIER :: SUNDAY VINYL, DENVER

Interaction with regulars and people in the neighborhood and community. The week of the tornado, so many people would stumble in for dinner, dirty and exhausted from volunteering in the neighborhood, and it's one of the things that makes me so proud to call East Nashville home.

—SHANNON WRIGHT :: TWO TEN JACK, NASHVILLE

Without a doubt what I missed most of all was having the ability to see all of your friends without even trying. Working, eating, and drinking around this town is a guaranteed way to see 95 percent of your loved ones, just by being out and about. I personally feel so much more creative when I am surrounded by like-minded people. It's very difficult for me to get inspired on my own. Almost as if I only get excited if I can get a group of people excited.

The hardest part about all of this has been seeing the effect it has had on my community. Ever since I moved here nine years ago, it has been *such* a positive and fulfilling place to live and work. Sure, we had bad nights at work and tough times, but there was always a friend behind a bar right down the street who would cheer you up in a heartbeat. A friend that would be ready to grab a bite to eat and drink one too many beers at lunch. And all of that could happen completely stress-free. Now I feel like so many people are glazed over. You can tell when you look in their eyes that they have seen some shit. The dark circles don't lie. You can tell the smile is a bit harder to put on—even through the mask, I can see it. Breaks my heart to know that so many people, myself included, are just feeling a bit overwhelmed.

—DRU SOUSAN :: HONEYTREE MEADERY, NASHVILLE

I never knew how much I truly enjoyed the social aspect of my job and how much it mattered to my mental health. Both coworkers and regulars alike. I miss people. And conversation. And hugs! Feeling closed off from friends and family is not something I ever thought I would have to experience, and it's been eye-opening and humbling.

—STEFANIE MARSHALL :: LOS ANGELES

HANKY
PANKY
p. 99

CHAPTER TWO

WE'D LIKE TO RECOMMEND...

(AND WHAT HELPED US THROUGH)

One of the great benefits to sidling up to a bar—next to drinking and connecting with other people—is getting all the carefully curated local recommendations from a passionate, undoubtedly opinionated barkeep. →

If you work in Nashville, two things are probably true: you're getting some tourists, usually with sore heels from clopping around in brand-new cowboy boots, and they want to know where to get this local delicacy known as "hot chicken," aside from the "this is our take on hot chicken" that's most likely on the menu you just handed them. However, the gift that keeps on giving is when a bartender, while also providing stellar hospitality, offers up music suggestions tailored to your tastes (while subtly expanding them), recommends books to broaden your mind, and movies and television shows that will get you binging in no time.

During quiet, contemplative times I enjoyed Akira Kosemura's masterpiece of a record, *In the Dark Woods*. Also on high rotation were the ambient keyboard compositions of Harold Budd, who sadly passed away from COVID-19 in December 2020, but not before releasing an absolute triumph of a record, *Another Flower*, which came out four days before his passing. Haim's new record, *Women in Music Pt. III*, really blew me away; the songwriting and the hooks are just amazing. In the "comfort" department, I enjoyed rereading Kurt Vonnegut's *Player Piano* and *Slaughterhouse-Five*, and Anthony Bourdain's fun and bizarre beach crime thriller *Gone Bamboo*. As always, I found comfort in absurdist humor, rewatching *The Campaign* (perfect for an election year) and episodes of *Curb Your Enthusiasm*, which keep me terrified and laughing hysterically at the same time.

What follows are the books, music, shows, and films we watched to get through this unique time. Oh yeah, and go to Bolton's for hot chicken.

Veep! Seven seasons on HBO and I crushed them in a couple weeks.

—EDDIE ADAMS

Bill Withers's *Live at Carnegie* has always been one of my favorite albums, but with his passing it made its way back into heavy rotation. "Grandma's Hands" is such a great song on the album. I love the intro with the story about the tambourine.

—LIZ ENDICOTT

Chris Stapleton, or Leon Bridges if I want to keep things mellow. I also might slip in some AC/DC if I need some fuel for staying active (which has been challenging while staying at home).

—ROBERT LONGHURST

I, like many others, have been devouring the '90s Chicago Bulls documentary *The Last Dance* on ESPN. It's a story about the drive and desire to win above all. I think, in such a weird time, with so much loss and uncertainty, it is a way to feel positive. I've also been listening to Jeremy Todd's (DJ Coach) Spotify sessions. He's making daily playlists with musicians, bartenders, and all sorts of Nashville residents. It's just one more way to feel connected with people you know in the era of social distancing.

—BRICE HOFFMAN

I am rereading the science fiction series The Expanse, which is probably as enjoyable if you are not a nerd but for different reasons. I am listening to Bill Frisell, a jazz guitarist who makes relatively simple music, with complex sounds.

—GRAHAM FUZE

I have been reading so many books about the era just after the Civil War up until the Great Depression. Doris Kearns Goodwin's new book, *Leadership in Turbulent Times*, is fantastic.

—CRAIG SCHOEN

Music gets me through most things. I've been listening to a lot of Stan Getz, Tchaikovsky, Mozart, Cigarettes After Sex, Nick Drake, Frank Ocean, Billie Holiday, some blues like Son House and R. L. Burnside. I don't know. It's my personality . . . all over the place . . . but it's all soul shit.

—ALEXIS SOLER

The Deuce on HBO was the first thing I committed to watching once things got locked down. It was fantastic in every way, and I was legitimately sad for a week when I finished the last episode. A very entertaining look into New York in the '70s and '80s, tons of grit, a little glamour, and far less polish. While I was happy to live there when it was safe to walk down the street at night, it made me wish I could have experienced some of that time, especially working in bars.

—BRANDON BRAMHALL

I kind of doubled down on the Hannibal Lecter canon. Rewatched many of the movies and the TV series, and am now delving into the books for the (embarrassingly) first time. The TV series *Dave*, about Lil Dicky, has also been a big topic of conversation for me. I have been in Arizona for the totality of quarantine, and found an old hard drive with my old music from high school and college, so I have rediscovered a lot of the underground hip-hop that I used to love. El-P and Buck 65 have been in heavy rotation. As for the song I've had stuck in my head the longest, "In Your Eyes" by The Weeknd just won't go away.

—ANDY WEDGE

I am such a sucker for trash TV. I think, like the rest of the world, watching *Tiger King* helped kill some boredom. I watched all four seasons of *Riverdale* and dragged a handful of friends down that path with me. Tons of great music came out, so that's been a big plus for me; American Aquarium (*Lamentations*), Jason Isbell (*Reunions*), and Gasoline Heart (*Big Trouble*) all put out amazing records, but the new Starflyer 59 single, "This Recliner," has been on repeat.

—JOSHUA "WOODY" WILLIS

I have been reading and reading and reading and shamelessly acquiring far more books than justifiable during this time. Fanny Singer's *Always Home*. M. F. K. Fisher's entire collection. Charles Eisenstein's *The More Beautiful World Our Hearts Know Is Possible*. For the first time in a long time, my life has kind of been characterized by show-watching (it's not usually something I allow myself to indulge in, as I have tendencies to obsess). We are now on the sixth season of *True Blood*, and if anything will remind me of the bizarreness and hilarity of this time, it will be the ungodly amount of hours we've invested into that show. As for music, anything that encourages movement, like "These Boots Are Made for Walkin'" (Nancy Sinatra) or "What's Wrong With Groovin'" (Letta Mbulu).

—VILDA GONZALEZ

My favorite show has been an accidental find on PBS called *Escape to the Chateau*. It's about a charming English couple renovating a four-hundred-year-old French chateau on a budget. Their humor and good-natured approach while taking on the enormous project is a delight to watch.

—JEREMIAH JASON BLAKE

I've been playing a fair amount of Dungeons & Dragons online to both stay in touch with people and get lost in another world. I've been listening to a lot of minimalist, ambient, post-rock, etc. It seems fitting for how quiet everything feels. Ólafur Arnalds's *Living Room Songs* is one of my favorites.

—MATT TOCCO

The book *Wine Simple* by Aldo Sohm. I'm trying to get back to basics. What does a sommelier look like in this new world?

Lefty Frizzell, "The Long Black Veil." I've been binging *Country Music* by Ken Burns and can't stop listening to Lefty!

—NICOLETTE ANCTIL

My favorite book of all time and especially during this time is *The Little Prince*—it is a celebration of the youthful perspective, the ability to value beauty and friendship over money, the reality that sometimes caring for something arbitrary or enjoying a sunset when you are sad are perfect ways to honor your own experience.

Ironically, I also read *Cat's Cradle* by Kurt Vonnegut (for the first time) and *The Bean Trees* by Barbara Kingsolver (for maybe the tenth time) during this pandemic—both have many bleak and bright moments, and despite the fractured world in each story, they convey hopeful messages.

I've watched a lot of movies while sheltered in place, and have enjoyed pairing them with cocktails. It's a unique challenge to find a cocktail and a film that evoke similar emotions, or make you feel even better when combined than either does on its own—just like the very best food and beverage pairings. They enhance each other; both are good already but significantly better when enjoyed together. The epiphany of a perfect pairing occurs when you discover magnificent characteristics in something because of its harmony with something else. My favorites so far have been *Joe Versus the Volcano* with the Jungle Bird, *Funny Face* with the Hanky Panky, and *A Simple Favor* with the Gin Martini.

—JESSICA BACKHUS

Books: *Garden to Glass* by Mike Wolf has been the latest addition to my shelves, and it has inspired me to start planning out an herb garden.

Shows: *Dead to Me, Workin' Moms*—really any shows that help me justify my wine intake right now.

Movies: I have recently rewatched all of the *Lord of the Rings* movies—the extended collection, so we're talking four plus hours each movie. And the original trilogy *Star Wars* movies. (I've been told these are the only ones that matter and I somewhat agree. Definitely not the last three.)

Music: Dolly! Yes, the beloved Dolly Parton has gotten me through a lot of down days, and she's even been perfect for the days I do feel like I'm on top of things. I've been mainly listening to her older albums: *Hello, I'm Dolly*; *Just Because I'm a Woman*; and *Jolene*.

I have also been listening to another one of my absolute favorite female artists again and again: a local Nashvillian, Alison Mosshart, from the bands the Kills and Dead Weather. If I was to contribute any song to your playlist, it would be her newest solo single, "It Ain't Water." It's perfect for any bartender and my favorite of hers at the moment. Her other solo single she just released is "Rise," and it's badass too.

—ALICIA SWARTZ

The show that has changed my life is *Letterkenny*. There's almost nothing funnier than Canadian culture, and I've always thought that it has something to do with the fact that everything is so similar to our expectation but usually with one tiny and hilarious difference. All I want to do is hang out in the yard with the boys and crush a couple of Puppers and blast off on some Gus N' Bru.

The last song I was jamming to on my drive home from my last shift was "My, My, My" by Johnny Gill. I've been riding this wave. Anything in the New Edition universe. The last track off their 1988 album *Heart Break*, "Boys To Men." I've always been a sucker for ballads. Nothing can ever beat that vibe for me. It's a good way for me to get emotional when shit gets really heavy, but these classic '80s power ballads are usually pretty uplifting while letting out the feels. Here's another perfect tune right now: "Through the Fire" by Chaka Khan.

—PAUL ROGERS

I rewatched all of *The Office* because I might be part Michael Scott and part Dwight Schrute!

Song: "Lavender," G Mills

Trippy as this time is, I heard this song early on in quarantine and have played it at the beginning of every bike ride and run I've done.

—ERIN BARNETT

Super Sad True Love Story by Gary Shteyngart and lots and lots of true crime documentaries. Some housemates and my fiancé are concerned about my rate of consumption of murder and intrigue, but I also remind him that I have better things to do than plot his murder.

—MERCEDES O'BRIEN

I really love sports and I have missed them desperately. Baseball is gone! I had Dodgers season tickets! The Lakers were rolling! Thank God for *The Last Dance*, which is informative, entertaining, but most importantly . . . it's sports. That has helped. I've started listening to more meditative and calming music at night because the grind can really get your head in a weird space. Jon Hopkins is an artist I really enjoy. I love the new Tame Impala album, and when all of this started, Kevin Parker released a different version of it called *The Slow Rush In An Imaginary Place*, (check it out on YouTube). It's awesome with headphones because you hear crowd noise and everything is kind of muffled, like you're hanging out in the green room area of a concert. Check it out!

—TRAVIS ARCHER

We've watched *The Americans*, and it is great. I also enjoyed *Hollywood* on Netflix.

    The records I've been most into have been:

    Richard Hawley, *Lady's Bridge*

    The Jayhawks, *Rainy Day Music*

    Also the general "This is R.E.M." Spotify playlist

    "Tonight The Streets Are Ours" by Richard Hawley is a winner.

—KYNSEY HUNTER

Mike Delfini made a playlist he called "Vibes" on Spotify. It's been a daily play, not only for me but for all of his friends and family as well. I've been listening to a lot of Bruce Springsteen, Creedence Clearwater Revival, Van Morrison, Aretha Franklin, and some jazz. Mostly Miles Davis and John Coltrane. All of these bring me joy and peace, especially on tough days.

—RILEY PERRIN ELLIS

I started and finished *Lamb* by novelist Christopher Moore and am on to *Noir* by him as well. His witty, unapologetic writing keeps my brain interested and allows me to escape in his books. I have revisited *Windows on the World Complete Wine Course* by Kevin Zraly, in which one of my favorite parts is the intro story about the now "Greats" in our industry getting their start and the boom of the hospitality and wine industry in the '70s, which Zraly then elegantly transitions into wine education that is—in my opinion—very retainable. As for music, it depends on the mood, task, weather, or even time of day. I have been listening to more reggae, as I find it tends to relax me, with its smooth beats and wailing melodies. Bob Marley is obviously a favorite, as well as Roots of a Rebellion.

—TARYN BREEN

Two books I've come back to during the quarantine are *Bitterman's Field Guide to Bitters & Amari* by Mark Bitterman and *The Dead Rabbit: Groceries and Grog, Mixology and Mayhem* by Sean Muldoon, Jack McGarry, and Jillian Vose.

—MATT BURNETT

I've watched a lot of *Kids in the Hall*. Currently reading *History of Madness*, though I don't recommend it during the quarantine. Music has been the best mood changer throughout my Lost Spring journey. My band broke up a few years ago, but I'm still writing, singing, and working on little projects. My obsession this week is mariachi. I really enjoy the full, deep, emotional quality of the vocals. I've made several playlists to help pass the time. The songs I've built the playlists around are "Cyber Sex" by Doja Cat (appropriate for obvious reasons), "I Wonder Where You Are Tonight" (the Dolly Parton version), "Oh Lonesome Me" by Don Gibson, and "Ojos Del Sol" by Y La Bamba.

I've been drawn to a lot of noir and horror films. As an interpretation of plague, *Dracula* really stuck with me. I noticed on rewatching it how Bela Lugosi as the Count never seems afraid, never seems concerned about being found out. He only draws closer, slowly, inexorably, like a sickness, first in a faraway country and then in the city and then with a friend and then in your living room, and even after they call him out, there isn't a whole lot anyone can do to stop him. They just have to wait for his time, the nighttime, to be over.

The twentieth century struggled with a lot of war, and the battle with this epidemic, in its scale and its loss, has many parallels. I've been finding comfort in a lot of film noir, especially Humphrey Bogart movies. There's something soothing and satisfying about watching this cynical, intellectual guy find his heart and fight his way out of a bad situation, in *Casablanca*, in *To Have and Have Not*, *The Maltese Falcon*, and *The Big Sleep*, among others. Alfred Hitchcock movies too—the creeping sense of dread, the relief of the unmasking of evil, the restoration of right in the world—is very satisfying right now.

I'm a musician, so I'm always listening to music as well. Not so much to tell me stories, but as an accompaniment to my life; to feel there is someone accompanying me, a companion, in my day-to-day struggles. The albums I've been listening to most this spring have been *A Love Supreme* by John Coltrane and *Déjà Vu* by Crosby, Stills, Nash & Young (CSNY).

The Coltrane I've been listening to for the breath. The way that he breathes into his horn and makes this sacred music. The way the other musicians support him. The way the breath becomes this holy thing. In this time of lung disease and ventilators, one can't help but think about how special a single breath is. Nothing emphasizes this more to me than the work of John Coltrane, especially this album. I listen to it while I'm running, and I try to breathe with Coltrane as he scales those bright peaks of song.

The CSNY I have been listening to for the way it responds with joy and power to the horror of the times of the late '60s. The sense of that era when the government expected people to die in Vietnam reminds me of this era when the government expects people to take the risk of getting sick to keep the economy running. The way those musicians responded to all the fear and horror of that time with "are waitresses paying the price of their winking while stars sit in bars and decide what they're drinking" and "I feel myself a cog in something turning, maybe it's the time of year, and yes maybe it's the time of man" are all really speaking to me now. and "are waitresses paying the price of their winking while stars sit in bars and decide what they're drinking" and "I feel myself a cog in something turning, maybe it's the time of year, and yes maybe it's the time of man" are all really speaking to me now. These themes of rebellion and sadness, of frustration and hope, carried by a loud, joyful rock and roll keep me going on dark days.

—LEAH SMITH

Right now I'm (painfully) revisiting *Brave New World* by Aldous Huxley.

—SALLY GATZA

I have been finding a lot of solitude in watching *The Sopranos*. I enjoyed listening to Nina Simone's *To Love Somebody* (that whole album). Fiona Apple's "Heavy Balloon" and "Ladies" songs have been playing on repeat. And you can't go wrong with a little J. J. Cale to start your morning. It just puts you in the right mood to get your day started and keep it going.

—ALI BESTEN

As far as cocktail and hospitality books, I read *Burn the Ice* by Kevin Alexander, and *Easy Tiki* by Chloe Frechette during quarantine. I have been listening to a lot of '90s club jams—thanks, Peloton, for the bangin' playlists!

—DEMI NATOLI

Books: In March, I read Christopher Cantwell's *She Could Fly #1*. My first graphic novel ever! It was amazing, and I love the format. April was poetry month, so I read *Wild Beauty* by Ntozake Shange. Highly recommend, but it has some intense subject matter. In May, it was *The Master and Margarita* by Mikhail Bulgakov. This book changed me forever. So great. Read that.

Music: Sunday Vinyl is a vinyl bar, so music is in our DNA. I love music obsessively. To spare you from a giant wormhole I could go down, I will give you one great music thing. I started a practice where I picked a song that made me feel special, really good, lifted. Listened to that song every day with my eyes closed and meditated on how I am good and loved, and warm, and a powerful being, and a being of light and energy, and alllllll of that while my song played. Try this and you will feel so amazing! My song is "I've Never Found a Girl (To Love Me Like You Do)" by Eddie Floyd.

—BRANDON ANAMIER

Lots of podcasts—*Armchair Expert* is a favorite; *Up First* and *The Daily* are also on my everyday list. We also picked movie trilogies to watch: *Indiana Jones*, *Jurassic Park*, and *Batman* (the Nolan and Burton versions).

—SHANNON WRIGHT

As a new small business owner, I have been reading books like *Marriage Without the Sex* by Rachel Schaffer Lawson. A great read for people just starting out or with years behind the wheel of a business. As far as music goes, the new Tame Impala album *The Slow Rush* has been one of my staples. It came out just a few days before the tornado hit, and for some reason, it has just been such a surreal album for me to listen to, now that the world is so different in such a short amount of time. Also, the playlists "Awesome Mix Vol 1 + 2" are some of my favorite Spotify playlists of all time! "Wham Bam Shang-A-Lang" by Silver from that playlist will put a smile on Dracula's face.

—DRU SOUSAN

The first half of quarantine, I had Harry Styles's new record on repeat—the song "Cherry" to be specific. It switched over to Kehlani's new album *It Was Good Until It Wasn't*. My favorites on that record are "Everybody Business" and "Open (Passionate)."

—STEFANIE MARSHALL

FANCIULLI

p. 99

THREE

TURN AND FACE THE CHANGE

When my friend Jessica Backhus turned me on to Honeytree Meadery last year, I remember thinking, "Damn, they're making craft mead in East Nashville, and it's actually good?" →

I said this while sitting on a swiveling red-leather barstool while gazing up at a sixteen-foot-tall robot . . . in a tiki bar. Yes, things have changed quite a lot over the last ten years in Nashville, and in the hospitality business in general. When I go back to Denver to visit family, driving down the one-way streets with timed lights, wondering "Is that shitty Mexican place still around? It was great," I come to find out it's now home to a new spot that's creating their own nixtamal with their own corn, making their own masa, and only serving animals who are massaged and bathed to early Genesis records. You even have to go out in the back and kill the chicken yourself. Okay, I made that last part up. But restaurants and bars have come so far over the last ten or twenty years that it's crazy and disheartening to see it all come crashing down in the span of a couple months. When I saw a statistic that potentially 75 percent of all independent restaurants may have to close by the beginning of 2021, I began to panic, wondering if Chili's was considered an independent restaurant. The end of Southwestern Egg Rolls? God help us.

Seriously though, independent restaurants are the lifeblood of our communities. They are the life force guiding us through our differences, feeding the heart and vice versa, providing nourishment and connecting everything around it. They bring us together, all while giving us even better takes on "Southwestern Egg Rolls." The people I have met and worked with in independent restaurants going back twenty-seven years (and I'm fortunate to have only worked in independent restaurants, fourteen total) are some of the most unforgettable, lovable, talented, hilarious, whip-smart people—you wouldn't even believe half of them were real. It breaks my heart to see so many restaurants, some of which were my favorite spots in town, close permanently during the pandemic. I've wondered where the restaurant and bar world was headed before all this. Was it about to buckle under its own ambition? Or was it about to turn a corner—or more accurately, bust through a wall—to a completely different era of equal pay, benefits for all, and psychological consideration for overstressed staffers? Things were starting to change. Now they are forever changed. But this is the industry of morphing on the fly, making it work, trying something different, and forging ahead when adversity strikes. What follows are some thoughts on how bartending and the industry might change moving forward.

There are a lot of germs in restaurants. We touch so many things. It's hard not to think about the changing of that postpandemic.

—SHANNON WRIGHT

The thing I really understand now is the value of bars and bartenders. It really is a thing that holds our society together. It wasn't the alcohol that everyone missed: it was the connection.

The humanity that happens over food and drink, being served, and doing the serving is all being undervalued. Hopefully everyone will understand now the true value of their favorite restaurant.

—BRANDON ANAMIER

A pandemic is definitely going to change the way the entire world experiences dining out. Currently I am changing the beverage menus. I am considering how many times we have to touch a cocktail before it gets to the guests—not as in "how many steps does it take to make this," but literally how many times will our staff touch something with their hands before the guest gets it. Who prepared the garnishes, and how many times was this lime touched? Did anyone touch this flower before I did?

—DEMI NATOLI

I feel I am more conscious about my approach because the restaurant industry has been hit the worst and was the last to get help. It's more "how can I be of assistance to you and your team, and what can we do together to move forward?" We've also

pivoted to selling hand sanitizer, and that has been an eye-opening experience to say the least.

—ALI BESTEN

I'll definitely be more thankful for a perfectly set up bar now that I've been making cocktails at home. I've always loved the guest experience, so I'll just be happy to get back to that and remember to savor it.

—SALLY GATZA

One thing I've taken away from all of this is that it's important to create time for yourself. I think everyone can get burnt out with whatever it is they may be doing, no matter how much they enjoy it. Once we're back to a somewhat normal lifestyle, I'll probably cut back a tad and just enjoy life a little slower.

—DEVIN DRAKE

I don't expect things to get easier very soon. These events will change my approach to bartending. My whole approach is to listen to and connect with people. It's hard to do that in a mask when you are afraid that they might make you or somebody else sick.

My last night of bartending was March 16, and although we were supposed to make sure there was six feet of space between each person, people kept coming in, and I kept letting them get closer. They were so hungry for company and laughter; I didn't have the heart to turn anyone away.

And more insidiously, in the back of my mind was the thought that if I was risking serious illness to be here, I might as well make some money. What's the point of exposing myself for ten hours to make $50? Then the man in front of me coughed. I said, "Did you just cough?" And he said, "Come on, I'm not sick, it was just a cough." What do you do? What can you say? He was one of my favorite guests, my first regular, and there was a newcomer there that night who seemed interested in him. Was I going to mess up his last chance to make a connection before the quarantine? Of course not. So I let it go. And I let another couple in, and another, until the bar was packed shoulder to shoulder. And all I could think was that someone here might catch it and be really sick or worse, and it would be my fault for facilitating this evening.

Usually I love facilitating an evening of companionship and merriment. It's what I'm good at. I'm decent at making drinks, okay at all the other required duties, but where I excel is creating an atmosphere of fun and friendship where folks feel welcome. How can I do that now? How can I welcome people to a place where they might get sick? Where they might get me sick, or cause me to pass it to a dear friend or treasured guest. How is anyone truly welcome in this circumstance?

—LEAH SMITH

It'll change everything for a while. I'm already used to washing my hands all the time and not touching my face, but the business itself has a fracture. We'll be nursing this wound for a long time, but we're a resilient bunch. I'm holding faith for us all. It's been really beautiful how everyone has come together to take care of each other. That will definitely carry over in how I continue my work.

—ADRIENNE STONER

I am interested to see how the industry will be affected. With certain bars and restaurants not being able to reopen, it makes me wonder about the process of workers finding new jobs in our industry. Before all this began, it was hard to find and hold on to talented staff. What happens now, when there are fewer jobs and the same amount of industry workers?

—MATT BURNETT

This has pushed me to be very introspective and grateful for the things I did not always enjoy or appreciate before. I want to be a better bartender and person every day, to have stronger relationships with my coworkers, where we can build each other up while always challenging each other to continue our education. Every guest experience will be cherished and savored as if it was the last service.

—TARYN BREEN

I do think this is a huge wake-up call for our industry. To reset our systems, our lifestyle, our mindsets. But does it change how I feel about bartending as a career? No. Now more than ever I believe we need to work together to save our bars and our restaurants. I believe wholeheartedly that bars and restaurants are essential to our world. We as human beings need places to go, to gather, to celebrate, to mourn, to meet, to decompress, to unwind. We as owners and employees in the hospitality industry offer that. We create our homes to share with others, so that they don't always have to stay in theirs. We do this because we love to serve people, we love to create, we love to indulge and enjoy delicious foods and wines and cocktails. And I don't think that will ever go away for us. Nor do I want it to. Now we just need to find new ways to do it.

—RILEY PERRIN ELLIS

It's really just uncharted territory. I have no idea what to expect with the "new normal," and I guess I'll adjust as necessary.

—KYNSEY HUNTER

I think when things start opening, you'll have to not just antici-pate a guest's basic desires for food and beverage, but also the optics of how cleanly and safely you work. Speed will eventu-ally come back, but I think we are all going to start off being as particular and attentive as possible, so the pace will be slower and more calculated. I don't think I will mind that—eventually the faster pace of days of yore will return—but until then, we can get back to basics. Plus, we will need to get our muscle memory and steps of service back. Shake and stir off the rust. But a shorter answer would just simply be "I have no fucking clue." I have been wearing masks and gloves at work for almost three months, and I have begun to notice some loss of dexterity, both when in gloves or just using my normal hands. This worries me a lot. My vision and hearing are kind of worse from masks, too, so I'm not sure how a blind bartender who can't hear anybody or feel anything is going to perform. Yeesh.

—TRAVIS ARCHER

It's made me take stock of my time and the way I approach bar-tending. I love going down off the beaten path and into experi-mental rabbit holes, but I realize people still want approachable but creative cocktails at home. Finding that balance for the pub-lic has been a new vision in my career path with SippN at Home, my new YouTube cocktail series.

—MERCEDES O'BRIEN

Interacting with so many people all the time can definitely wear down certain aspects of your personality, so I always try to come back from a break with fresh energy. People are going to need that energy. I'm definitely hoping that everyone on both sides of the bar comes back humble, with some perspective on the things that really matter. I've lost a couple of friends during this time. It seems a little dramatic or cliché, but you never know when you're going to talk to someone or serve them for the last time. Giving as much love as you can in every interaction might make a big difference, and I never quite understood that.

—PAUL ROGERS

As much as I love my regulars and the rush of a Friday night service, I really want to slow down, experiment more, take my time with each ingredient, learn, and create. I wish to only create and conceptualize right now. If you know me, you know I am one to appreciate the fine details of service, but I think I've decided that I'm finished with the service aspect and being in front of the guests. I would like to focus more on personal growth.

—ALICIA SWARTZ

It's going to be more challenging than before, but more rewarding as well.

—NICK THAXTON

Despite the perception that our industry has always been a precarious one, it wasn't until this pandemic that our future was truly in jeopardy, that the threat of *Demolition Man*'s "franchise wars" and emergence of just one restaurant with one way to eat became so close to reality.

As restaurants reopen with fractional capacity and a limited number of people coming in the door, I am hopeful that I can create memorable experiences on a more intimate level, but I am terrified of the instability of that prospect. How do you limit your offerings, reach a smaller audience, create something magical, and still get exposure when so much depends on financial success? Maybe I should have been reading *Catch-22* during the quarantine . . .

—JESSICA BACKHUS

I had already felt that it was becoming too hard to teach young bartenders the basic building blocks of bartending. Everyone wants to work at the newest places, and the newest places are normally trying to do something, well, new. I hope this allows us time to go back to the basics.

—MATT TOCCO

While the way we serve may change, my approach to bartending won't change that much. I'll still be excited to see you. I'll still make you the best drink I can. I should probably work on my bar jokes though.

—JEREMIAH JASON BLAKE

I think our hospitality as a whole is finding new ways to ensure our guests as well as our employees are safe and responsible while still maintaining a fun atmosphere. Hospitality 201's main focus is events and cocktail catering, so we are working hard to find new ways to do the same. The hospitality industry is no stranger to having to make quick changes, and we always make it through even better than we were before.

—CARLEY GASKIN

I'm not sure where I first heard it, but someone told me no matter what happens in the world, good or bad, bars will be safe because happy or sad folks will want to drink. I learned that's not true and to really appreciate what we have as a community and not take it for granted.

—JOSHUA "WOODY" WILLIS

We are going to have to relearn how to do pretty much everything to make sure that safety is always number one moving forward. Thinking about spacing and where we stand and work behind the bar is going to be a big part of that.

—ANDY WEDGE

It's likely going to alter some of the logistics of how we do things, like making drinks, serving drinks, the flow of service, and the additional things that we'll need to provide to makes guests feel comfortable and confident in our cleanliness and safety. Unfortunately, it probably won't make things easier, but we're highly adaptable in hospitality. New challenges can only help us sharpen our skill sets and approach to caring for guests.

—BRANDON BRAMHALL

How do we help humans that are having all these extreme and traumatic experiences restore joy and comfort in spaces outside of their homes? That is where we need to put in the most work.

—ALEXIS SOLER

Change? Hopefully not. I simply want to be in the hospitality business again.

—CRAIG SCHOEN

I have even more respect for our role in the lives of the people who sit with us. I want to ask them more questions and share the best of my self.

—GRAHAM FUZE

I think we took a lot of stuff before this for granted and didn't realize how quickly it could change. I don't really know how that is going to manifest itself until we reopen and start to see the lasting impacts this has all had. And when it does, we'll move and adjust and find a way to create something new and hopefully familiar at the same time.

—BRICE HOFFMAN

Safety and cleanliness are always top of mind for any good bartender, but I think unique approaches that limit touch points during prep are going to be key. Batched cocktails or frozen machines using fresh, prebottled juices and ingredients might be something to think about. A six-step cocktail that requires the bartender to touch every ingredient, including the fruit or herb garnish, might not be as appealing as it used to be.

—ROBERT LONGHURST

The biggest thing that changed for me is ensuring our guests have plenty of affordable options. I don't believe we have really felt the effects the quarantine will have on our economy. Cocktail culture is fun and ever-changing, but the price of a good drink has gotten pretty high.

—LIZ ENDICOTT

Guests are going to be hyperfocused on the sanitation and cleanliness of the restaurants. I'm going to have to be extra aware of what I am doing behind the bar and whether or not my actions will look bad to those coming into the restaurant. I'm going to have to slow down and make sure I'm not being lazy with anything.

—EDDIE ANDREWS

As far as my sanitation goes, I can honestly say that not much of my bartending practices will change. I have always been a huge advocate of being extremely sanitary behind my bar, for both myself and my guests. When all this COVID-19 talk started, I was not one of the worried bartenders wondering if they had it or not. I felt very confident in the fact that my cleanliness had given me a good chance of staying safe. As far as interacting with my guests, that may change no matter how much I try to deny it. Being such a vocal and social person to everyone is not necessarily the safest thing these days. Am I going to put that same extra effort into a long and meaningful conversation with a guest that I would have had before COVID? I hope the answer is yes. I hope that during those interactions I do not feel worried about how close someone is or if they are wearing a mask or not. With the tasting room still being closed I have not had those interactions yet and am very curious as to how they will feel.

—DRU SOUSAN

FOUR

THERE'S NO WHINING IN WINE

One of the things I noticed about the wine program in my house during this pandemic, especially early on, was that quantity ruled over quality. →

That's not to say I wasn't enjoying some decent wine from time to time (I've practically made it a sport to find the best wines under $14 for most of my adult life). It's just that I needed plenty of variety around, as colder nights shifted to pink wine evenings, and that post-mowing beer suddenly became a book club-sized glass of Vinho Verde. Here are some thoughts on wine when times are tough, starting with my homegirl Jess Backhus's amazing pairings for frozen food.

Here are some of my wine pairing suggestions with frozen food.

- CHEESEBURGER, STEAK-UMMS, ETC.: **Sparkling wine! Traditional method rosé is great, preferably not cava—the bubbles are usually too sharp, and it can have a sort of coppery flavor that is aggressive for the beef.**

- BAGEL BITES, PIZZA, RAVIOLI-TYPE FOODS: **Nebbiolo and northern Italian blends; non-classified stuff is usually delicious and cheap. Also, Sangiovese and chianti-type blends are good.**

- CURRY, INDIAN-SPICED TRADER JOE'S MEALS, AND SUCH: **Pinot blanc, Edelzwicker, and other Alsatian blends with a beautiful balance of aroma, fruit, and mineral.**

- COTTON CANDY-FLAVORED ICE CREAM: **Pinot noir. It sounds weird, but just trust me.**

If you're looking for wine on the cheap, here are some other suggestions.

- BUBBLES: **For traditional method sparkling wine from parts of France other than Champagne, Crémant de Loire and Limoux can be great and inexpensive. Traditional method sparkling wines from the US can also be delicious, especially when they're on sale—Gruet from New Mexico is a diamond in the rough!**

- WHITE: Look for wines from the Loire Valley in France or from northern Italy, and try different ones from Slovenia and Croatia—a great way to get into orange-type wine without paying too much!

- RED: Spanish reds give you the most bang for your buck and pair well with almost anything you eat. Dry, dusty Tempranillo and Grenache from northern Spain (even entry-level Rioja), bold and defiant Priorat from the northeast, and dark, rich, juicy wines from the south are usually delicious.

—JESSICA BACKHUS

Frozen pizza and sparkling red wine. It's the perfect mix of class and trash. I think an excellent way to try out wine without someone walking you through it is to find importers that you trust. That way, you can have some confidence that what you are buying is of a high quality. Vom Boden and Fifi are two of my favorites. Lastly, find wine from places that you might not be familiar with. If you want pinot from Burgundy and cabernet from Napa Valley, you're going to have to pay the price tags associated with those regions. But if you can get off the beaten path, you can find some truly incredible wines for fractions of the price. One of my current go-to's is from Austria. There are a ton of great, responsibly made wines coming out from tons of great producers.

—BRICE HOFFMAN

For your everyday pairings, dry rosé and affordable bubbles are pretty awesome with almost anything and can be found at good prices. From someone who has sat on bottles past their prime in the past, waiting for the perfect moment that may never come, I recommend opening that special bottle sooner rather than later.

STRAWBERRY
ROSÉ
CHAMPAGNE
COCKTAIL
p. 129

But make a day of it. Find a difficult or special recipe that will pair well with that wine, commit to cooking something outside your comfort zone, and savor creating something yourself that goes with a bottle you have been saving. Extra points if you do it on a random Tuesday night to make what might be an otherwise mundane day into something to be remembered.

—ANDY WEDGE

Springtime always means rosé time. I'm sure we are all enjoying some canned soup, so why not pair tomato soup and grilled cheese with a nice bottle of Château de Trinquevedel Tavel Rosé? Retail stores have done an awesome job with creating "bundles," allowing for guests to access wine at a lower price. I think we can be better consumers and use our purchased wine to get a little more creative. For example, a bottle of cava can go a long way—drink it on its own, or make a French 75 or a Tuesday Mimosa brunch. Whatever your daily theme may be, cava is there to help you on the cheap. I've really enjoyed the virtual tastings I've found here in Virginia; connecting with the local winemakers has been a true gift.

—NICOLETTE ANCTIL

I've learned that Pizzolato merlot goes with whatever the hell you want.

—ERIN BARNETT

Trader Joe's has the best frozen section, with meals that are delicious and some that are even restaurant quality. Bounce over a couple aisles and boom! The best wine deals ever! I love the Pontificis Rhône-style white blend—swirled together are viognier, roussane, and marsane, all for $7. With a fuller mouth feel, white flowers, medium acidity, and a juicy finish, it's great paired with seafood, poultry, pasta with butter or cream-based sauces, or, honestly, just on its own.

—TARYN BREEN

SPICY
MEZCAL
MARGARITA
p. 127

FIVE

BLOOMS OF THE LOST SPRING

(SILVER LININGS IN DARK CLOUDS)

It can be very difficult to find a silver lining in dark clouds when they're all stitched together overhead, in differing shades of gray, blanketing the sky like an old quilt left out in the rain too long. →

At least that's what it started to look and feel like in the spring of 2020. An uncertain future seemed set on becoming the dark, dystopian dream Kurt Vonnegut laid out in *Player Piano*, where machines had taken over much of the workforce, the skies were always gray, and the insiders and outsiders were wondering if there was any green grass to be had on the other side. But hey, if you're looking for a silver lining, at least machines are shiny! Stories started to drift out, real or imagined (the line more and more blurry), about restauranteurs in New York City preparing to replace bartenders, dishwashers, and *maybe* that moody server named Dani by robots, mobile sanitization units on wheels with the cold calculation to cut overhead, eliminate mistakes, and, you know, stay open. But for all of us who were confined to our living spaces, holed up with our families, or living in more loneliness than all the country songs of Nashville, there *were* plenty of things to be thankful for.

My garden never looked better, my hedges were trimmed with Edward Scissorhands–like precision (for a couple weeks anyway), and my pets never seemed happier. Though after a full month of staying in the house, my cat, Boone, began to look at me with a stoic skepticism that said "Are you just going to read the paper all morning? Don't you have anything better to do?" My dog, June, would stare at me wide-eyed, saying "These kids are driving me nuts, can you tell them to stop laying on top of me?" That's right, my pets were starting to talk to me. Though it can be tough to parent two small children through a pandemic, when they can't see their friends or hug their grandparents, I felt very fortunate to have my kindergartener daughter back at home full-time. I had missed our random backyard sessions, swinging in a hammock in the middle of a Monday morning. Eventually, she, too, began to tire of the quarantine, though it was entertaining to watch a six-year-old look up at the sky and shake her fist, screaming "I hate the coronavirus!" It was also a pleasant change to not be tag-team–parenting for a while, where you get stuck in a cycle of handing off the baton and saying "You got this, gotta go!" Life had slowed, and as parents, we were better for it. What follows are more thoughts about the positive side of staying home for a long while.

Well, I've actually had pretty positive experiences during this whole thing. For one, it's been super nice to drive without people on the roads. I've also been fortunate enough to have had the opportunity to work on a peach orchard during the shutdowns. It's been beneficial for my mental health to just go and escape the fear of these times. I've also learned so much about agriculture as well. The peaches, as cheesy as it sounds, saved me from a potentially dark period of my life. Getting a little bit of cash didn't hurt either.

—EDDIE ADAMS

Spending more time with my family, slowing down, and enjoying being at home with my little one. The past two years have been hard with a young child. Hrant and I were in a constant state of panic during the quarantine, but we had so much fun being together as a family.

—LIZ ENDICOTT

Seeing the formation of groups like Tennessee Action for Hospitality and Independent Restaurant Coalition has been very encouraging, and I hope these groups can work with local politicians to find something to fairly support these struggling businesses that have had no choice but to close their doors. Seeing the average bartender find creative ways to make cocktails at home has also been great to see.

—ROBERT LONGHURST

Slowing down has been nice. My wife and I were both furloughed, so we have had an absolute abundance of time to hang out. We've never had that. With the exception of yearly vacations and trips, we have been working full-time since our relationship started. Being able to take that time and just be together has been great. Also, our animals are in absolute heaven with us being around all the time.

—BRICE HOFFMAN

I have appreciated the quiet time, getting up earlier, and doing more mindful practices.

—GRAHAM FUZE

Quality time to reflect on what is truly important. I had hoped that the politicization would dissipate, but . . . not so much.

—CRAIG SCHOEN

Learning to slow down and take better care of my mental health has been a gift.

I have relearned that sometimes the path created for you was made with a boulder blocking the way. It's a time to stop and step back, slow down, and reflect. What is on the other side is unknown, and who you are on the other side may be different. That is what excites me in all of this. Life is fragile and can change at any time. LOVE while you are here.

—ALEXIS SOLER

I got some really good sleep for the first time in three years. I have taken up backup hobbies I rarely had time for before we opened Attaboy in 2017 that have been a great outlet to cope with not just COVID, but also with the aftermath of the tornado. Gaining new perspective, as well as taking an honest stock of what's most important in life, has been a good reset to my approach to everything.

—BRANDON BRAMHALL

I have been in Arizona this whole time, staying with my mom in the house that I lived in through high school. With all the moving around I have done over the years, I haven't always done a good job of keeping in touch with or taking care of her. I am thankful for the fact that I have been around to help out during this time.

—ANDY WEDGE

I finally found time to tackle some projects around my house, mostly making my front yard look like an actual yard. I officially learned the importance of the "after-a-mow beer."

—JOSHUA "WOODY" WILLIS

I'm blessed for feeling called and empowered to share what I'm best at sharing: food as love. Spending more time with my man, nurturing a wild and erratic garden, and having the abundance of time to wander and dream.

—VILDA GONZALEZ

I've been able to reconnect with several hobbies I've lost over the years, such as photography and painting. My dog has never been happier having both parents at home all day!

—CARLEY GASKIN

A renewed joy with life's simple pleasures. I've been constantly reexamining this idea and reminding myself of the abundance around me. It's been my best defense against becoming over-whelmed by everything thrown at us recently.

—JEREMIAH JASON BLAKE

Plenty of time to exercise, meditate, and read without feeling like I should be doing something else.

—MATT TOCCO

I've found tremendous creativity during this time; the quiet has been difficult and also fueling. I've been thinking about teaching people about wine on completely different platforms. I really enjoyed connecting with nature and seeing the earth grow.

—NICOLETTE ANCTIL

The best thing about staying home has been spending all of my time with my person, Lauren. She is the most talented baker, cook, collaborator, friend, and partner, the best palate, the greatest supporter, and the most graciously honest critic I could ever hope for. Some day we hope to combine our business dreams and goals and share our talents, passion, and creativity with people on a professional level. During the quarantine, we've made amazing meals and drinks, enjoyed wines, and experimented with recipes and ideas that we've always had but never had the time to really try out. This has given us the chance to do it all and to ponder all of it together. It has been incredibly liberating and inspiring learning to adapt, get creative, use whatever resources we have, and let go of the craving for instant gratification that's embedded in us as Americans.

I've also begun to teach myself to fish. Now that I can go out into nature at any time rather than just when the weather is good on my day off, and due to the facts that I'm surrounded by amazing aquaculture resources and that sitting in a kayak is a perfect form of social distancing, I'm determined to start bringing home the catch of the day so we can enjoy sustainable seafood on a regular basis.

—JESSICA BACKHUS

I've had many blessings. I recently moved to East Nashville and planted my feet here, along with an herb garden. My relationship with my girlfriend, Tasha, is as strong as it's ever been. I've also spent many fun hours laughing and playing Xbox with my best friend Garth and my brothers.

—NICK THAXTON

One positive thing that has happened during this time is that I have been able to spend more time with my father. We've talked more about life and feelings than ever before. He's been teaching me about gardening, birds, and astronomy. Another positive is that I have been able to connect in new and positive ways with friends. I've found that when social obligations are removed, I've been able to focus on what matters most: health, relationships, and personal growth. I now have the time to take that hour-and-a-half long walk, or FaceTime a friend for hours, or watch movies and read books all day and not feel guilty. Every day I have found it easier to be more productive and to try new things. Like my shrub-making, cooking, and jogging. I'm not sure I would've made time for these things in my old day-to-day life.

Lastly, I was let go from my job. I know this seems like a negative, but I could tell I had started to grow unhappy. After we were told we could open the dining at 50 percent capacity, I offered to continue my managerial duties, but I wasn't comfortable with being in front of guests, and I knew they weren't taking many precautions in the beginning of all of this, which automatically made me feel uncertain and unsafe about my returning. I was denied and fired without even a conversation. I worked there for a year and a half; I was a part of the opening staff. I only bring up the details of this because it directly deals with COVID-19, and I know others in the industry who are sadly experiencing the same thing. I don't expect jobs in our industry to come without work, or for any management role to be easy; I've been in this grind for sixteen years. But I'm a true believer in teamwork and supporting one another and building a community in a positive work environment. I also expect managers or owners in any business to reach out during a global pandemic and care about their employees' well-being. Value and self-worth are two things I don't take lightly or for granted. Because of this, I have had to force myself to think about what my future looks like, whether it be in or out of the hospitality industry, even though it's the only thing I've ever known. It's a hard and scary thing to do.

—ALICIA SWARTZ

I'm the type of cat that likes to go really, really hard in the paint. I shifted my entire focus to posting up in the studio and growing my business there as a producer. I've realized that game is basically a service industry as well. It's my job to take artists and songs and bring them to life in the way that they intend. Also, a shout-out to Erick Castro (San Diego). He is always encouraging artists to make sure they stay creative in multiple outlets. When I get burned-out working on cocktail menus, a little time whipping up a couple tracks in the studio totally rewires my brain. I feel like I've been able to stay creative and continue to help people, and hopefully I'll be able to take those vibes back to the bar and get to the next level there as well.

—PAUL ROGERS

I have been able to attend a lot of webinars that producers have felt the need to do, and I have learned a lot from them. I have been able to catch up with friends that don't normally take the time to have a phone conversation. I have learned that the people I work with are amazing and worth the time I put in.

I've also had time with my kid that I'm so grateful for.

—ERIN BARNETT

I took the leap to start a dream project with my fiancé (oh, and I got engaged) called SippN at Home. SippN at Home is a cocktail platform focused on creating and sharing cocktails using everyday household ingredients, bringing a dose of hospitality "from the corner of our living room to yours." Each episode lends professional insight and techniques to the at-home bartender who can expect a heavy sprinkle of hacks and fundamental knowledge for relaxed accessibility, with no intimidation or worry. Cocktail kits are available as well so that viewers can shake along.

—MERCEDES O'BRIEN

I've enjoyed learning different skill sets at work, making more time to check up on friends both here and afar, and a sense that inherently good people are probably going to come out of this as better, more well-rounded people that will combat the shitty people that got worse. Being able to provide food for people in need is great, and there is a certain reward for seeing their appreciation for your work. That being said, I haven't had much time to relearn how to play the trombone or work on some writing projects or try new and interesting things. My situation is relatively unique in that regard. And when restaurants open, I will just go right back into it. I need a vacation!

—TRAVIS ARCHER

This quarantine forced me to really address some issues and projects I had been avoiding. I couldn't make excuses or procrastinate as much as I usually would by using my job as an excuse.

—KYNSEY HUNTER

The only thing I can say after all of this is that I now truly and deeply know how much love, support, and friendship I DO have in my life. I have the best friends and the best family anyone could ask for. I am forever grateful for them; they're my blessings. And this forced time to slow down has not been an entirely bad thing. It's allowed me to take a step back and analyze and prioritize my life in a way that suits ME. Not other people. I've been working five to six days a week, long and late hours for seven years now. While I wasn't expecting this, nor was I really asking for it, I'm extremely thankful for this time to slow down, to rest and reboot, and to plan what's next. And of course, Mike's forever-lasting words, which I will continue to spread near and far: positive vibes only.

—RILEY PERRIN ELLIS

Since I'm fortunate enough to live where there is warmer weather, I have been lucky enough to do more hiking, kayaking, and planting in these few months than I have done since I started working in this industry twenty years ago. Every part of my body has also been able to rest and reset in a way I have not experienced since I was a child. Also, I appreciate this opportunity to be featured in a book with people I respect and look up to.

—TARYN BREEN

The best thing to come from this quarantine has to be the time I've gotten to spend with my wife, Savannah. Being in this industry, I have, on multiple occasions, gone a few days without time to spend with my wife. She would wake up for work before I wake, and I would get home from work after she fell asleep. This would sometimes continue for a few days at a time. People joke that spending all this time with their significant other might be a strain on their relationship, but for us, it's been amazing.

—MATT BURNETT

During this time of uncertainty, I have been able to get away from the city. I jetted off to southwest Florida, where I've spent lots of time fishing and being with family. Having all this time off from the industry has been hard but also a blessing. It has definitely helped me understand why I got into the business in the first place. I, for one, have not stopped serving people; I've been cooking and making drinks for family every day and night.

—NICK DROHAN

I've really been able to focus on my health and hopefully have a new approach going back to work. One of the hardest things about this industry is how badly it can affect your health, and I've really been able to take the time and figure out how to deal with that going forward.

—SALLY GATZA

Finding the motivation to improve every day has been a challenge. However, the time has really helped me be still and look within, and I think that is a positive.

—ALI BESTEN

Outside of financial difficulties, it has been interesting to be alone with my thoughts. I have diagnosed anxiety and depression; falling into a slump was something I actively worked against every day. I am really fortunate that I have a trail by my house that almost nobody uses, so I tried to work on myself and exercise, which I really hope to continue doing.

—DEMI NATOLI

Despite feeling like a candy house melting in the rain, I found a lot of peace during my time alone at home. It was the first time I was able to experience spring weather and be off of work to enjoy it. Granted, I couldn't leave my backyard, but just the feeling of the sun on my skin before it became 95 degrees every day, and the insect-less nights—that was pretty amazing. I was able to spend time thinking about what I want out of different aspects of my life, what and who is worth my energy, and who I want to be for other people. We all get caught up in our pointless shit so often we forget what's worth our brain and heart space. The tragedy felt by so many during the tornado, pandemic, and human rights movement during this time has been more than we ever thought we could endure. But, as a community of bartenders, as a community in Nashville, and a community of humans who exude empathy and compassion, we are fucking pushing through and making big moves. I'm excited for the future.

—KELLY GABLE

I don't feel like I lost my spring at all! I deepened my spiritual quest, strengthened my body, fed my mind, and learned a few new things. I really just pushed myself to stay in a routine every day, never allowing myself to become too bored. Looking back on a three-month journey, I can see progress in so many areas beginning to take hold. I hope to continue to weave this energy back into my work routine.

—BRANDON ANAMIER

This has totally been a time to slow down, reflect, and nurture yourself.

—SHANNON WRIGHT

I have learned how to reflect. How to take a breath—like a legit, calm, meditation breath. I have gained a new love and respect for being a small business owner (shit is no joke). A half-decent garden at the house! And an increased awareness of how amazing Nashville is. My motto for this time period is: we may not have it all together, but together we have it all.

—DRU SOUSAN, HONEYTREE MEADERY

Somehow, I have saved money! Which goes to show just how much money I sunk back into nonessential businesses (and fellow bartenders' pockets). I've also been able to focus on writing and have made considerable progress on a novel I've been trying to write for a long time. It's not done, but it's something close to progress.

—STEFANIE MARSHALL

I made dumplings for the first time! I've been able to spend time talking to old friends. My great-grandmother and I have had some fun chats. I'm making small progress in my French lessons. People have brought me dinner. I've taken road trips just to stare into the lake. The struggle is separating my self-identity from my work. In the end, I realized that I do this work because it's in my blood. I'm excited for the changes we're facing as an industry. Natural forces have sort of forced our hand. We will have to grow and evolve into something stronger, kinder, and more connected. It's an opportunity to be better. We adapt and overcome.

—ADRIENNE STONER

What will these next few years bring? The good thing that has come out of this is that I've had so much time to work on creative projects. I have always been an artist, a writer, and a musician, but my bartending job takes a lot of my energy and enthusiasm. It was difficult to have anything left when I got home to work on my own projects.

Now I have time for a different focus. I am never bored; I am always busy. There aren't enough hours in the day for me. I run, I do yoga, I meditate. I try and find some space to breathe. Right now, I am playing guitar for hours and writing songs for an album for the first time in years. Also, I am writing a murder mystery novel. I hope to have time to start painting again. It's fun to be creative in these other, more solitary ways.

Although these pursuits might make less money than my job, they have more tangible results. There is an incredible amount of creativity required to facilitate a beautiful evening. To make sure everyone has a good time, that stories are told, that the night is memorable, that all participants are appreciated and satisfied, that the food and drink comes out properly, and that all is paid for appropriately can be a Herculean task. But there is no proof of your work other than the money you make. Now, how satisfying it is to have a body of work, songs and stories written down, that last forever, instead of each ephemeral evening fading away like a puff of smoke. Like dandelion fluff blown in the wind.

—LEAH SMITH

MARTINI

p. 97

SIX

COMFORT BOOZE AND NINE ESSENTIAL COCKTAILS

A perfectly griddled grilled cheese.
Tomato soup, simmered to just the right
amount of thickness. →

The combination of the two, the cheese even more gooey after emerging from the slow dunk into the soup, now for the textural, umami-blasted sensation of biting into the crusty, grilled bread, partially softened from the soup, and the blast-off flavor affinity of tomato-cheese-hot bread—Is this just deconstructed pizza? I wonder in a state of dopamine food-buzz hysteria—hitting your taste buds, lighting them on fire, but most of all . . . telling you it's going to be okay. Like Mom used to make, on a cold day in early spring. I sat there enjoying this comforting combination early on in the isolationist stages of "Quarantine 2020," wondering what my cocktail equivalents were. The answer, as for many of us rethinking the rituals of making drinks at home, was right in front of me: a cold coupe from the freezer cradling a dry martini with three olives, floating like picturesque Icelandic hillsides among cool, clear waters. Don't worry, I can keep going, turning this into a cologne commercial featuring former James Bond, Pierce Brosnan, swirling around a half-drunk martini while sporting three rings on each finger and gazing up at the gargantuan, rocky coasts of Iceland, while someone whispers "refreshingly different." But I'm here to talk about the drinks and spirits that comfort us during prolonged stretches of adversity, when the mere act of staring at a clock that reads "4:47" and watching it slowly meander its way to "4:59" as you reach for the mixing glass is its own bit of mental mountain climbing.

Many bartenders I know, and for a long time I was firmly in this camp, don't really go to much trouble making cocktails at home. For many of us working in any mildly high-volume situation, the idea of coming home and cranking out yet another drink, even if this one's for the all-important "ME," seems to take the fun out of both making drinks and gulping them down. Cooks don't come home from a long shift of crushing three hundred-plus dinners only to whip themselves up a wood-fired beet salad. They open up a bag of Doritos and confront the existential dilemma of "Why is this bag of Cool Ranch Doritos slightly better than the third caviar-driven course at that amazing tasting menu I experienced in Chicago last year?" Bartenders throw back a shot or two of well whiskey and slurp on a beer, wondering "Is Tecate Light necessary?" But desperate times call for thoughtful drinks, and so many beverage professionals went from "tequila is my home bar" to "I really do need a better at-home vermouth program." Whether a carefully considered original creation, the ever-present "riff" on a classic from the cocktail canon, or a streamlined "this is what I've got in my liquor cabinet" topped with soda, making better drinks at home started to become a way of life for many of the cocktail creators who, prepandemic, presided over the full-blown renaissance of the modern cocktail.

If I'm working in a bar or restaurant situation, I love utilizing fresh citrus, back bar curiosities, garden and pantry items like tarragon, basil, or fancy sea salt, and creating memorable drinks for people based on their own preferences or cocktail dreams. "I love a Mai Tai but you probably can't make that," or "Can you make me a take on a Margarita?" are a few of my favorite recent requests. At home, I've always enjoyed the bare bones classics: Manhattan, martini, Old-fashioned, Negroni. Over time I became the curmudgeon, cursing otherwise fine establishments for their inability to craft the pristine, bracingly cold classics of my own cocktail dreams. "How hard is a Negroni?" is a question many bartenders have wondered to themselves while posted up at bars that bear only one similarity to the sidewalk cafés and Negroni temples of Italy: cracking sidewalks on the patio. So my home bar setup soon became a pared-down inventory-takers dream of sweet and dry vermouths, gin, rye whiskey, Campari, fernet in the freezer (for when the second helping of lasagna is stretching the limits of my "jogging pants"), a bottle of Maraschino Liqueur which takes forever to finish, and a few ubiquitous bottles of bitters. Sure, I've got some fun homemade bitters and tinctures lying around, but now is not the time for showing off! The only citrus needed for many of these cocktail mainstays is for the delicate swaths of orange or lemon peel, used for aromatic bursts of brightness and for the most basic of fancy flourishes on a drink: the twist.

There was something comforting about the fact that I could make many of the absolute treasures of cocktail lore with this simple setup, utilizing

the maple syrup from the fridge for sweetener from time to time. The beautiful thing is you don't even need a set of shaker tins for these mini masterpieces, as these are all "stirred" drinks. Remember when James Bond was always saying "shaken, not stirred" regarding his martini? Well, he was full of shit. For nearly all of these drinks (I'll dive into the Manhattan and the Old-fashioned in detail in the next chapter), you fill a mixing glass or a pint glass with ice, add your ingredients, stir for a good long while until the drink is well chilled and then let it all sit there on the counter, undisturbed, like you're resting a steak. After five to six minutes of literally chilling out on the counter, the drink is ready. Pour into a very cold glass, garnish simply, sit back, and enjoy the classics that will always be with us.

MARTINI

2½ ounces Plymouth Gin

¾ ounce good dry vermouth (Massican, La Quintyne, Dolin are all great examples)

1 or 2 dashes orange bitters

Stir, let sit to rest, serve up in a martini glass with a lemon twist and a few olives.

MARTINEZ

1½ ounces gin

1½ ounces sweet vermouth (a lighter French style vermouth would work well here)

1 teaspoon maraschino liqueur

1 dash Angostura bitters

1 dash orange bitters

Stir, let sit to rest, serve up in a martini glass with a lemon twist.

OLD PAL

1½ ounces rye whiskey

1 ounce Campari

1 ounce dry vermouth

Stir, let sit to rest, serve up in a coupe, and garnish with a lemon twist.

NEGRONI

1 ounce gin

1 ounce Campari

1 ounce sweet vermouth (Massican, Dolin Rouge, or Cocchi Torino would work well)

Stir, let sit to rest, serve on the rocks, and garnish with an orange slice and an orange peel, expressed over the drink and inserted. To combine the flavors of these two Campari drinks, try making a Boulevardier, and swap the dry vermouth in the Old Pal for sweet vermouth. I guess that makes this "Ten drinks to master"? I can see the men's magazines now.

HANKY PANKY

1½ ounces gin

1½ ounces sweet vermouth

¼ ounce fernet (Fernet Branca, Leatherbee Fernet, and Leopold Bros. are all good choices)

Stir, let sit to rest, serve up in a coupe, and garnish with an orange twist.

FANCIULLI

2 ounces rye whiskey

¾ ounce sweet vermouth

¼ ounce fernet

(optional) 1 dash of Angostura bitters—it really depends on the sweet vermouth of your choice. The fernet should suffice in terms of bitterness and spice, but if you opt for a sweeter vermouth you may want to experiment with adding a dash of aromatic bitters.

Stir, let sit to rest, serve up in a coupe, and garnish with an orange twist.

TORONTO

2 ounces rye whiskey—Sorry, Canada, but we want American rye for this one, which requires a higher percentage of rye grain in the recipe (at least 51 percent compared with 10 percent for our friends to the North) of the whiskey. You want to taste that spice of the grain, otherwise why are you drinking rye (said the curmudgeonly bartender)?

¼ ounce fernet

Scant ¼ ounce maple syrup

Small piece of lemon peel, no pith

Stir ingredients, being careful not to over-agitate the lemon peel, which will release more bitterness. Let sit to rest, serve up in a coupe, and garnish with a lemon twist.

MANHATTAN

(detailed description, page 106):

2½ ounces rye whiskey

¾ ounce sweet vermouth

2 dashes Angostura bitters

1 dash citrus bitters (anything from Dram to Regan's Orange)

Stir, let sit to rest, serve up in a coupe, and garnish with an orange twist and a cherry (or three, if you're my wife).

OLD-FASHIONED

(detailed description page 111):

2 ounces rye whiskey

Scant ¼ ounce maple syrup

2 dashes Angostura bitters

1 dash citrus bitters

1 small piece of orange peel (the size of a coin)

Add the peel, bitters, and maple syrup to the mixing glass without ice and lightly muddle together to form a concentrate. Then add the ice and the whiskey and stir until very cold. Let it rest for 5 minutes, as with the others, and strain into a rocks glass over however many ice cubes make you happy, and garnish with a cherry and an orange peel.

If you love classic cocktails and enjoy the simplest of drinks, these recipes will give you plenty of joy. They are also the perfect template for
exploration, an unintended gift from the cocktail gods when it came
to the "mother recipes" and the drinks that would follow. For example,
try substituting ANY ingredient in these drinks for Green Chartreuse,
Bénédictine, any sherry you can think of, or an amaro from Italy that
speaks to you, and you will have completely different—but delicious—
beverages in front of you. During the initially dreadful days of quarantine
when the news only seemed to get worse by the day, these were my
comfort booze staples, steeling the nerves, bracing me for the further
unexpected, and for my wife, an emergency room nurse working on
the front lines, these cocktail rituals became our time to slow down and
remember: we had each other, we had our incredible children (he said
through clenched teeth while fumbling for tomorrow's lesson plans), our
pets, and *lots* of time on the back porch. And the soup was just beginning to simmer. Now, about that Manhattan . . .

SEVEN

MORE ON MANHATTAN AND THE OLD-FASHIONED

When you start talking about
a perfect Manhattan, things get
confusing pretty quickly. →

There is only one "perfect Manhattan," made with whiskey, equal parts dry vermouth and sweet vermouth, along with bitters, and yet there are so many ways to make a Manhattan, enough to convince yourself it *is* the perfect cocktail, and it can be hard to decide on that definitive recipe. The recipe you'll keep coming back to when the nights are cold, the fire is burning (literally or figuratively), and all you need to completely change your life for fifteen minutes is one good drink. Like many of the "canon cocktails" on which modern drinks are based—think Negroni, Old-fashioned, Daiquiri—the Manhattan has three ingredients: whiskey, sweet vermouth, and bitters, garnished with a cherry. There are so many variables at play in a good Manhattan, but a great place to start is the whiskey itself.

The first element you want to start thinking about when deciding on the perfect whiskey for a Manhattan is proof. Many of the whiskeys sitting on the shelf at your local wine and spirits shop are bottled at 80 proof, a common denominator for everyday pours like Jack Daniel's, Jim Beam, and Four Roses, to name a few. But this level of strength just isn't going to cut it in the ideal Manhattan, which has to contend with—and cradle—the bold flavor profiles of sweet vermouth and bitters. You want a whiskey that is at least 100 proof, since you'll be stirring your drink until it is well-chilled and diluted, and you still want to have plenty of body and weight to the finished product. Rittenhouse Rye, Wild Turkey 101 (bourbon or rye), and Old Weller Antique 107 proof, made with wheat, are fine choices for a silky sipper. Which brings us to the flavoring grain, and the decision: bourbon or rye?

Since the original Manhattan was concocted with rye whiskey, it has become common for bartenders to reach for rye when crafting this classic. But it's more than historical accuracy that makes rye the ideal choice. The spice backbone inherent in many rye whiskeys happens to blend amazingly with the actual spices used in aromatic bitters and sweet vermouth. If you taste a young rye whiskey, say between two to four years old, you'll pick up some lovely vegetal and herbaceous notes, like dill and fennel. But as the rye ages in the barrel, the mild spice of the rye grain begins to take on more spice from the barrel and you're left with a spirit with a pleasant "bite" to it, begging to be made into a cocktail. Rye is even the flavoring grain for most bourbons, often contributing up to 20 to 30 percent of the total recipe. If you insist on using bourbon for your Manhattan, look for a "high rye" bourbon like Four Roses Single Barrel or Redemption's High-Rye Bourbon.

For a softer spice note, albeit one with a delicious character all its own, look for a "wheated" bourbon, which sees the rye flavoring grain replaced by wheat. Some examples include the aforementioned Weller 107 and Maker's Mark, which has recently released its 101 proof version previously available only at the distillery in Kentucky. Call it one of the few blessings of the pandemic. Now, if you're reaching for a wheated bourbon for your Manhattan, it's time to take a close look at which vermouth you'll be using. Since wheated whiskeys generally have a milder, more nuanced flavor profile, try a French sweet vermouth—like Dolin or Noilly Prat—which have light herbal notes and are less intrusive than their bolder Italian counterparts.

Though there are plenty of differences between the most widely available Italian sweet vermouths, one thing they share is an audaciousness, with the ability to assert themselves in the simplest of drinks. The chocolate and fig notes of the velvety Cocchi di Torino can be gorgeous sidled up next to an aged whiskey and some spiced bitters, while the vanilla and marshmallow lusciousness of perennial favorite Carpano Antica can make even the blandest whiskey seem top shelf. But therein lies the conundrum in choosing your vermouth. If you reach for something bolder than the flavor of your whiskey, you'll have a good cocktail, but it won't be the pristine, perfectly-matched Manhattan of your dreams. If you find the vermouth overpowering the whiskey, try dialing back the vermouth in the recipe by a quarter ounce at a time. To master this matching game of whiskey and vermouth, experiment by tasting them side by side and see if they complement each other or share any similar tasting notes. The most powerful of all Italian sweet vermouths, Punt e Mes (meaning one point sweet, a half point bitter) is absolutely delicious on its own and is a great choice in creative cocktails when you're searching for a lingering bitterness. But it is too overpowering in a Manhattan, which is all about balance, texture, technique, and harmony. The bitter snap of Punt e Mes seems to negate the use of bitters in a Manhattan, which brings us to your easiest decision: Angostura bitters. By any other name, the bitters would actually be . . . well, still bitter.

Though Angostura are the tried and true mainstay of the Manhattan as it has meandered its way through history, there are plenty of other delicious options to tie together the almighty whiskey and vermouth. Cocktail instagrammers would laugh at the simplicity now, but ten years ago, people thought they were being revolutionary by adding orange bitters into Manhattan riffs all over the country. Orange peel is an ingredient in many Italian bitters and vermouths, and the affinity between oranges and Manhattans is such that it is common practice for a bartender to express the oils of an orange peel over the glass as the last step of a well-made Manhattan. But take this cue and try adding a light dash of citrus bitters in your Manhattan, and see if the lingering bright note of acidity, contrasting with the deep barrel and spice notes of the whiskey and vermouth, are scratching that itch for the ideal Manhattan, which I present:

LDEAL MANHATTAN

2½ ounces rye whiskey

¾ ounce Italian sweet vermouth (Cocchi di Torino)

1 dash orange bitters

2 dashes Angostura bitters

Cherry and orange peel, for garnish

Stir ingredients with plenty of ice until well chilled. Then let the drink sit in the ice undisturbed for 5 minutes (find your exact sweet spot, depending on the proof of your whiskey). Next, strain it into a chilled coupe glass (straight from the freezer), plop in a cherry or two, and finish by expressing an orange peel over the drink and around the glass. Discard the peel. You've made it to Manhattan Mountain.

DON'T CALL ME OLD-FASHIONED, JUST MAKE ME ONE (HE SAID TO HIMSELF)

How can it be that the name of a drink could be so righteous as to be nostalgic, timeless, and perfect, all while being deemed "old-fashioned?" It's the ultimate paradox of the drinking world. The name itself comes from bar guests in the 1880s declaring—and I'm paraphrasing without period dialogue here—"just make it the old way for me, make it old-fashioned." They were even nostalgic back then, the suckers! But how amazing it is that this simple mixture of bitters, sugar, spirit, and water—the essence of what a cocktail was at the beginning and what it remains now—is still one of the most popular drinks whether at a bar or making drinks at home. Just as with grilled cheese and tomato soup (see previous chapter), there are all kinds of variables at play with the Old-fashioned. If you've ever had a bad one, it sticks in your mind. What possibly could have gone wrong in such a simple request? Too sweet? Forgot to add bitters? Too much ice, or not enough? Luckily for the home bar imbiber, many of these mistakes can be fixed on the spot. But the devil remains in the details, and there are some little tricks that will make big differences in your Old-fashioned game.

THE CITRUS PEEL

A small piece of orange or lemon peel—and we're not talking about the garnish, but we'll get to that—can be the key element to adding complexity to your Old-fashioned. When incorporating this step, execution is key because you don't want to add any unwanted bitterness to the drink. You're already getting that level of spice and bitterness from the bitters themselves. Simply take a Y peeler—an indispensable tool for the home bartender—and carefully peel off a small piece of orange or lemon peel (orange is most common and harmonious) about the size of a quarter. This small step is worth practicing because if you dig into the fruit too much, you'll get too much pith (the white part) and end up imparting bitterness into your cocktail. However, if you enjoy real bitterness in your cocktails, utilizing pith is a great way to add intense, fresh bitterness into the equation. But that's another story and a different drink. You're going for a very thin piece of citrus peel that, together with the sugar and bitters, is going to make up your Old-fashioned "concentrate." The tiny bit of citrus releases the bright, floral aroma in the peel into the drink and brightens things up, adding a lovely contrast to the bold flavors of the spirit and bitters. With an Old-fashioned, you're going for harmony, to make any middle-of-the-road spirit into something magnificent. Anybody can drink whiskey on the rocks or mezcal straight, and god bless those who enjoy the simplest of things in the simplest of ways, but an Old-fashioned is a ritual, and if you can master it, you're on your way to mastering other classics. An Old-fashioned can be a unifier in the beverage world since almost any spirit, nestled in the proper way to showcase that spirit's own unique flavor, can be made into a delicious beverage, all while appreciating what it is that makes the spirit unique. Since we worked from the pared-down maple syrup version of the home bar in chapter 6, let's look at a two other ways to do an Old-fashioned. One with wheated bourbon and lemon, and another as a bottled Old-fashioned you can pull right out of the fridge and pour over ice. Why lemon peel with the wheated bourbon? I once asked Julian Van Winkle III, grandson of Pappy Van Winkle, keeper of the Van Winkle whiskey tradition, and in charge of the most famous wheated bourbon on the planet, "What's the ideal way to drink wheated whiskey?" He replied, "In my family, we like it on the rocks with a lemon twist." Consider the matter settled.

WHEATED OLD-FASHIONED

2½ ounces wheated bourbon (Maker's Mark 101, Weller 107, or Bernheim Wheat Whiskey)

¼ ounce sorghum or maple syrup

2 dashes Angostura bitters

Small piece (coin size) of lemon peel, no pith

Combine the lemon peel, bitters, and sorghum or maple in a mixing glass and lightly muddle to release the oil in the lemon peel. Add a full glass of ice and the bourbon and stir gently until well-chilled. Let the drink sit for 5 minutes, then strain over a big ice cube in an Old-fashioned glass. Ponder your next Old-fashioned riff.

BOTTLED OLD-FASHIONED

GOOD FOR ONE 750 ML BOTTLE

I also love this bottled version to take on camping trips or to pull out when entertaining a few friends outside by the fire. It may take the ritual out of making an Old-fashioned, but it sure is easy to enjoy.

16 ounces Bourbon or Rye

7 ounces water

30 dashes Angostura bitters

6 very thin orange peels, as little pith as possible

1 ounce maple syrup

Combine whiskey, water, bitters, and maple syrup in a large bowl and stir to combine. Strain into an empty 750 ml bottle, add the orange peels, and cap the bottle. Stored in the refrigerator, the bottled Old-fashioned will keep for months, but I doubt you'll need that long to finish it. To serve, pour 3½ ounces over ice in a rocks glass and garnish with an orange or lemon peel.

CLEAR ICE AT HOME

One thing we've all missed from cutting-edge cocktail bars, while we bide our time making drinks at home, is the crystal-clear ice that has become so common in modern bars. The cloudy ice cubes we're all accustomed to in our own homes *can* allow some off-flavors to affect the taste of those final sips of your drink. When I was at Husk, we were buying clear ice from an ice sculptor and hacking away at it to get these beautiful, rocky diamonds that we could use for high-end whiskey pours and premium cocktails. After a while, the cost of the ice just didn't make sense anymore, and we couldn't use the excuse that "we've just opened, so we don't have the means yet to make our own clear ice." I did some research and began some trial and error, finding that the key to clear ice is allowing plenty of time to let the ice freeze slowly, allowing the impurities to form at the bottom of the container you're using to freeze the water in.

The easiest way to pull off clear ice at home is to fill a small Coleman-style cooler with water (it does not need to be boiling, just straight from the tap). Place the cooler with the top *off* in the freezer and wait a day or two for your ice to slowly form. After a day or two take the cooler out of the freezer and let it sit on your counter for about twenty minutes to warm up enough so you can extract the block of ice from the cooler. Set some towels on the counter for the inevitable mess of melting ice. When you've extracted the ice from the cooler by turning it over and letting it slowly drop out, use gloves and a serrated knife to "score" the ice, making it easier to break up into whatever shapes you want. You can find ice picks specifically for cocktail ice on Cocktail Kingdom's website and at some kitchen supply stores. Be careful when breaking down ice! I've seen plenty of people cut themselves, and I've even poked myself a few times with an ice pick. Take your time, and through trial and error you will have crystal-clear ice diamonds in no time.

GARDEN
GIMLET

p. 122

EIGHT

GARDENTINED COCKTAILS AT HOME

As the summer of 2020 rolled on and
the number of cases continued to climb,
I found solace in one of the places
I always have—the garden. →

I was finding a good balance between growing vegetables to use in everyday dishes and experimenting with things I had never grown before. Job's tears, a grassy plant that produces a bead-like seed and is perfect for making jewelry, was a lot of fun to grow. I also found a good balance with my squash, as I picked the male blossoms to use in salads and to turn into fritters filled with mascarpone cheese. They were insanely delicious! While I got into the rhythm of picking these male blossoms—the ones which protrude from the plant with their own stem attached, rather than the female blossoms which stay close to the vine and produce delicious squash—my squash plants were more productive than ever. This was a great lesson to learn as I'm always wishing squash season would last a little longer in the summer. What follows are some fun drinks I made during the spring and summer months using the garden and nature's bounty.

GARDEN GIMLET

As you start to enjoy the milder temperatures of September nights, the fact remains that there are plenty of warm days left on the calendar, before a glass of whiskey or a Hot Toddy by the fire are calling your name. I've found myself outside even more as the stifling heat has given way to those golden afternoons we only dream of in the dog days of . . . three weeks ago? It's that tweener season where you might be scratching your head on the porch, wondering "I should make a cocktail, but what should it be?" Maybe you've got some herbs in the garden, flourishing in the fresh, mild evenings. Since you've been through a LOT these past few seasons, you're undoubtedly hiding some gin in the liquor cabinet. Enter the ultimate blank canvas for making delicious drinks with a few fresh ingredients: the Gimlet. Invented to ward off scurvy and ensure that British sailors would actually drink lime juice, the Gimlet is also the perfect antidote to SEYD (seasonal election-year disorder).

The Gimlet is fascinating historically as it's actually pretty difficult to recreate the original, seaborne sipper. Sailors were drinking a concoction of gin and preserved lime juice, essentially an early, homemade version of what would become Rose's Lime Cordial, the neon green, corn syrup–laden midcentury mishap that's probably gathering dust in your parents' or grandparents' liquor cabinet. In those original nautical Gimlets, sugar was added to lime juice to preserve the flavor, but one can only guess what other tasting notes were present in those drinks. A little salinity from the ocean air, drifting over the hull as waves crashed all around? Sounds lovely. Some funky, wild yeasts making their way into the preserved lime juice? Not so lovely. Thankfully, you only need a few ingredients to make a drink so refreshing and inviting that you'll be tweaking it for all seasons. I like adding some basil and a little squeeze of grapefruit juice to my late summer Gimlet, as the basil in the garden this time of year is flowering, and a few of those tiny buds can add so much flavor when shaken into your cocktail. Is it already getting cold where you live? Try a fall Gimlet using a barrel-aged gin like Ransom and a light dash of Angostura bitters to introduce some fall spice. As I write this from Nashville, it's 90 degrees out and the dogs just want to nap near the air-conditioning vents. By sunset it will be much cooler, and I'll be thinking about making another Gimlet.

GARDEN GIMLET

2 ounces Bristow Gin (or any herbaceous, botanically focused gin)

¾ ounce fresh lime juice (usually the amount of juice in one lime)

¾ ounce simple syrup

¼ ounce fresh grapefruit juice

5 small basil leaves (or flowers if you've got 'em!), one of which will be saved for garnish*

Add all ingredients to a shaker, tearing 3–4 basil leaves just before adding them in, saving one basil leaf for garnish. Add ice to your shaker and shake until very cold. Double strain your drink into a coupe and garnish with one basil leaf and any other flowering herb or aromatic herb from your garden, as long as you know it's edible.

*If you don't have any basil, parsley would be a great substitute here. You can tailor whichever herb or vegetables you have around and shake them up in a Gimlet. Cucumber dill Gimlet? Lavender honey syrup Gimlet? Rosemary and a little shot of lemon juice? The possibilities are multitudinous.

WATERMELON PALOMA

I love the late-summer harvest which seems to pour into the markets here in Middle Tennessee. It is a great time to drink tequila and watermelon together. September is known as "harvest month," and the perennial late-summer star known as watermelon is offering much-needed refreshment at the table. With its floral aroma and unmistakably juicy texture, watermelon conjures summer memories like the smell of barbecue drifting through the neighborhood in July. It's also incredible in cocktails. This recipe is a twist on the simplest of drinks from the Mexican cocktail canon, the Paloma.

Traditionally a bare-bones thirst quencher involving a little lime juice, a salted rim, some tequila, and a healthy pouring of grapefruit soda—usually Mexican Squirt or Jarritos Grapefruit—the Paloma invites reinterpretation as there are so many other ingredients to pair with these essential, tequila-friendly flavors. And the cane sugar–sweetened taste of these sodas, while insanely delicious, can easily make your cocktail too sweet and unbalanced. My Paloma remix combines zero-sugar grapefruit sparkling water with a light agave nectar (you can also substitute honey), which helps give the thin watermelon juice and the ensuing cocktail more body and depth. Basil thrives in the late summer to early fall window and would be a great addition to this drink.

If the thought of breaking out that vegetable juicer you never use just for the sake of wringing out a little watermelon juice gives you anxiety, one way to easily juice your watermelon is in the blender. Simply cut a few large slices of watermelon, slice the fruit from the rind—which can be pickled to amazing results by the super-sustainable—add a few tablespoons of water, and blend for about 5 seconds. Strain your watermelon juice through a tea strainer (to strain out the seeds) and you're ready to go. Now all you need to do is rinse out the blender and give this recipe a try.

WATERMELON PALOMA

2 ounces TC Craft Blanco Tequila (or any decent silver tequila)

1 ounce watermelon juice

¾ ounce fresh lime juice

¼ ounce light agave syrup*

Basil leaves or mint, for garnish

Grapefruit sparkling water (La Croix and Bubly are a few brands that could work here) to top

Add all ingredients to a blender and blend with 8–10 ounces of ice for about 6 seconds. Pour into a tall glass with a salted rim and top with grapefruit sparkling water. Garnish with basil or mint.

*If you don't have agave syrup, you can substitute a quick honey syrup made by heating up 1 ounce of water and 1 ounce of honey in the microwave or on a stovetop. Stir the syrup and let it cool slightly before using it.

SPICY MEZCAL MARGARITA

With the news breaking that eating hot peppers can prolong your life, why not shake a few into your favorite cocktail? Capsaicin—the chemical compound found in chili peppers which has been shown to decrease inflammation and regulate blood glucose levels—is now being lauded for its potential to lower the risk of dying from cardiovascular disease or cancer, according to research presented at the American Heart Association's Scientific Sessions 2020. If there's one drinking trend that I've noticed take hold over the last few years, it's the proliferation of spicy peppers being used to liven up cocktail standards like the Margarita and the Bloody Mary. One of the benefits of using peppers for cocktails is the relative ease with which you can incorporate them. A few small slices of jalapeño shaken into a cocktail can give so much flavor and heat, leaving you with plenty for another drink, or the ability to use the rest for dinner that night.

There are a few ways to make your peppers last longer, as the weather becomes colder and fresh peppers at the market become scarce. One is

to make a hot pepper tincture. You can start by cutting peppers in half (wear gloves if you're working with hot peppers!) and drying them in an oven at 200 degrees for 1–2 hours, before adding them to a mason jar of 100 proof vodka. One easy ratio would be 1 part dried peppers to 2 parts vodka, but make it stronger if you have a high tolerance for heat. Keep the jar in a cool, shady cabinet and shake the mixture every day for a few weeks. Once the tincture tastes strong enough for your liking, strain the mixture through cheesecloth, squeezing the solids to extract as much flavor as you can, bottle the tincture, and use it within six months.

Another way you can stretch out the flavor of peppers and use them in cocktails is by infusing them into a light agave syrup. Simply pour a bottle of agave syrup into a nonreactive saucepan and add either fresh or dried peppers and simmer slowly over low heat for twenty minutes. Remove the pan from heat and let it cool with a top on. Transfer the syrup to a container with a tight-fitting lid and infuse overnight in the refrigerator, or longer for a more intense flavor. Strain the mixture into a clean bottle, store it in the refrigerator, and use within a month. To make your syrup keep longer in the refrigerator, add 1 ounce of vodka or tequila as a preservative.

Though these methods can allow you to stretch out your ingredients and limit waste, there's no easier way to add a little kick to your cocktail than by throwing a few slices of hot pepper directly into the shaker. One tip I can offer: use a separate knife and cutting board for your spicy peppers so you don't accidentally leave a few screaming hot pepper seeds sitting on the counter or permeating your everyday cutting board. And if you're using cayenne or jalapeños, you may want to use gloves, and remember to wash your hands thoroughly when you're done.

I love mezcal—tequila's stronger, smokier cousin—to add to this recipe during the fall months, as it gives a warming feeling when mixed with bold peppers. The Aleppo-salt rim adds to the complexity and mixes well with the vibrancy of a spicy cocktail.

SPICY MEZCAL MARGARITA

1 ounce mezcal

1 ounce blanco tequila

¾ ounce lime juice

Barspoon (⅛ ounce) orange juice

Scant ½ ounce agave nectar

Tiny pinch of salt

1 slice of jalapeño (plus 3 more slices for garnish)

1 sprig of dill, for garnish

Aleppo-salt rim - 1 part salt and 1 part Aleppo mixed together (substitute chili powder if you don't have Aleppo)

Rim the glass you'll be drinking from with the Aleppo-salt mixture and set aside. In a shaker tin, combine the tequila, citrus, agave, salt, and 1 slice of jalapeño. Add ice and shake until well chilled. Double strain (through a tea strainer or other sieve) into your salt-rimmed glass over ice. Garnish with 3 small slices of jalapeño and a sprig of dill.

SHERRY COBBLER

The first time you try a Sherry Cobbler, one of the first cocktails to achieve widespread popularity and the reason why straws became part of our drinking toolkit, you'll wonder how you ever lived without it. Since it's so low in alcohol, this is the ideal drink to dream away an afternoon in the summertime. The key here is to use really thin citrus peels and plenty of summer fruit for garnish, giving you something to snack on while you sip this drink in a hammock.

> 3½ ounces Manzanilla sherry (Fino or Amontillado would be fine to substitute)
>
> 1 thin orange peel (as little pith as possible)
>
> 1 thin lemon peel (as little pith as possible)
>
> 1 teaspoon sugar
>
> 1 dash Angostura bitters
>
> Citrus slices, berries, and mint, for garnish

At the bottom of a shaker, muddle the citrus peels, sugar, and bitters gently to release the oils in the citrus peels and incorporate them with the sugar. Add the sherry and ice and shake until well chilled. Strain into a julep cup filled with crushed ice and garnish with citrus slices, berries, and mint. Serve with a sustainable straw.

STRAWBERRY ROSÉ CHAMPAGNE COCKTAIL

This simple, fruity delight is a great way to combine the flavor affinity of strawberry and dandelion without getting too complex in execution or presentation. It's an absolute crusher when the sun is out.

1 strawberry, top removed and sliced into 1-2 inch pieces

1 dash Angostura bitters

5 ounces Sparkling Dry Rosé

Dandelion flower petals, optional

In a flute or other wine glass, add the diced-up strawberry and one dash of bitters. Top with the sparkling rosé and garnish with dandelion flower petals.

DANDELION ALASKA

The martini is such a home bar mainstay in my house as it fills the role of the cocktail unifier. If my wife and I can't agree on what's for dinner or which wine we should open, we can always agree on having a martini. Nothing quite alters a late afternoon like its cold cradle. But sometimes you're out of olives and have a tiny bit of yellow chartreuse hanging out in the freezer and feel compelled to make the most elegant riff on the martini ever created. The Alaska cocktail is essentially a martini that gets herbaceously bolstered by the addition of yellow chartreuse. In the late spring, when dandelion and forsythia flowers are blooming all over the yard, they make for a fantastic and functional (yellow chartreuse smells like dandelion) garnish for this sophisticated sipper.

1½ ounces gin

½ ounce yellow chartreuse

½ ounce dry vermouth

1 dash orange bitters

2 dandelion flowers, 2 forsythia blossoms and a lemon twist, for garnish

In a mixing glass add one dandelion and one forsythia blossom, the dash of bitters and the yellow chartreuse. Very lightly muddle to extract some flavor from the blossoms. Add ice and the other ingredients, and stir for until well chilled. Let the drink sit undisturbed for five minutes and strain into a chilled coupe. Garnish with a dandelion flower, forsythia and lemon twist.

RAMOS AT HOME

The Ramos Gin Fizz wasn't supposed to be the most difficult drink to pull off. Don't listen to anyone who tells you to shake this drink for five to ten minutes. I use half and half in mine—rather than the more common heavy cream—because half and half is something I keep around for coffee and almost always have it in the refrigerator. It makes for a lighter and fluffier drink that is the closest you'll ever come to drinking a cloud of gin.

1½ ounces gin

1 ounce half and half

1 egg white (as fresh and local as possible)

½ ounce lemon juice

¼ ounce lime juice

½ ounce simple syrup

2-3 ounces soda, for topping

3 drops orange flower water (optional), for garnish

Mint, for garnish

In a shaker tin, combine all ingredients and shake without ice to fully incorporate the egg white and the half and half. Add one or two ice cubes and shake robustly for a few minutes. Strain the drink into a long, tall glass and let it sit for about thirty seconds to allow the head to settle. Then top with soda and garnish with 3 drops of orange flower water and sprigs of mint.

TROPICAL SWIZZLE

When it's tiki time and you haven't spent hours and hours making your own falernum and orgeat, this is a simple way to get tropical without spending too much time prepping. Taylor's Velvet Falernum is easy to find at local liquor stores and is very affordable for how flavorful it is. Add a few spices from the spice rack and you're basically on island time.

2½ ounces aged rum

¾ ounce lime juice

¼ ounce orange juice

¾ ounce Taylor's Velvet Falernum

1 dash powdered cinnamon

1 dash powdered allspice

3 dashes Angostura bitters

Orange slice and mint, for garnish

Add ingredients to a tiki mug or other drinking vessel and fill the vessel halfway with crushed ice. Swizzle briskly with a swizzle stick (pictured) or a long bar spoon until the ingredients are mixed and the drink is frosty cold. Add more ice to fill. Garnish with mint and an orange slice.

DON'T FORGET ABOUT THE BAMBOO

While this one was a "project" cocktail created with the vermouth I made with Love and Exile wines (more on that in the epilogue), it's also a fairly simple riff on a classic from another era, the Bamboo Cocktail. I encourage you to seek out different unique vermouths and singular sherries to come up with your own Bamboo riff, which is just dry vermouth and sherry, with a hint of bitters.

> 1½ ounces Garden to Glass Dry Rosé Vermouth
> (substitute Cocchi Rosa, or any other dry vermouth)
>
> 1 ounce Manzanilla sherry
>
> 1 dash Angostura bitters
>
> 1 dash citrus bitters
>
> Edible flowers, for garnish, optional

Stir ingredients with plenty of ice until chilled. Strain into a coupe and garnish with edible flowers, or a lemon twist.

LAVENDER SAZERAC

I love a good Sazerac and appreciate the simplicity of this drink, which has stood the long test of time. However, when I cut some lavender from the garden to use in the vermouth I was making, I randomly decided to tear off a piece and try it lightly muddled in a Sazerac, which can come off as a tad medicinal. The combination of fresh floral aromatics along with the bouquet of absinthe coating the glass was a revelation. I encourage anyone growing things and making drinks at home to completely improvise like this from time to time. Do you have lemon balm taking over a corner of the garden? Try adding 10 leaves of lemon balm to a sweet tea and bourbon. Fresh herbs don't need much cajoling to take a drink from basic to bold and beautiful.

> 2 ounces rye whiskey (preferably something in the 100 proof range)
>
> Scant ¼ ounce maple syrup
>
> 2 dashes Angostura bitters
>
> 2 dashes Peychaud's bitters
>
> Absinthe, to rinse the glass
>
> 2 sprigs lavender (1 for garnish, 1 for muddling)
>
> 2 thin (as little white pith as possible) lemon peels

In a mixing glass, add one of the lemon peels, one of the lavender sprigs, maple syrup, and bitters. Gently muddle everything together, then add the whiskey and the ice to the mixing glass. Stir until well chilled and let sit for five minutes. Rinse the glass you'll be drinking out of with absinthe. Gently roll the absinthe around to coat the

glass and discard any extra absinthe. Pour the drink into the glass and serve neat. Garnish with a lemon peel, expressed and inserted into the glass, and a sprig of lavender.

NINE

A CLOSE-UP OF THE HONKY TONK

BY MATT CAMPBELL

FORMER SECURITY, SINGER, AND BOLOGNA SANDWICH
SLINGER, ROBERT'S WESTERN WORLD -SPRING 2020

I'm sufficiently immersed in warm
water, frothy with Good Dreams coconut
bath powder, drinking a glass of cheap
Italian red wine. →

The scent of a vanilla candle delicately mixes with the last notes of a stamped-out joint, and Linda Ronstadt sings "Blue Bayou" through the Bluetooth speaker resting on the edge of the porcelain sink that reflects the flickering candle.

I must have heard that song four hundred times between the different female singers on the stage of Robert's Western World, from the weekly regulars to guest singers, or the bartenders taking a short break for a small star turn. Sitting here in Warsaw, I still get ready to sing in unison, "I'm going back someday."

Working at Robert's was like being in a special club that enjoys some status, the value of which became clouded or clearer depending on the day, the number of dollars involved, and a desperate need to exploit the most valuable of skills: willingness.

When I got the job as a barback, one daytime a week, I offered open availability to the then-manager, Julie Rahimi. She fired back, "What are you doing tonight?"

I had done only one shift during a slow December when I received my first paycheck, but along with it was a Christmas bonus bigger than my day's wage. When Julie asked me if I could cook, I didn't think twice before saying yes. I did tell her that it had been nearly twenty years since I spent a spring break and a couple summer months as a short-order cook in a neighborhood bar as a teenager. Good enough. She needed a grill cook for New Year's Day, and she was looking deep into her bench to find a warm body. In hindsight, I can fully appreciate her attempt at reassurance, insisting that the day after such a big party would be slow and manageable.

When I arrived early that morning, the floor was covered in trash, cups, cans, napkins, and paper food trays. By the time eleven o'clock rolled around, I had done a modest amount of prep while the small cleaning

crew returned the room to ready. The day bartender, Hope, had arrived and was bouncing between the bare tables, setting up menus, ketchup, mustard, and salt and pepper. The first band had filed in and was hitting a few obligatory notes to test the sound system. That was it.

For about twenty minutes, all went as planned. A few stragglers staggered in as the door was propped open on a crisp January day, but it seemed most of the town had decided to sleep in. I even had time to practice my technique for making the house favorite: a fried bologna sandwich.

What makes the Robert's version so special are the thin slices of bologna. Put six to eight of them directly onto the flat-top. Two slices of Texas toast follow, each generously buttered for purposes of taste and toasting. Flip the bologna halfway between the golden-browning of the bread, time enough to slice a tomato and get a thick leaf of lettuce to lay the foundation for the simplest, and still decadent, delicacy in all of downtown. Add a few dill pickles or a Kraft single if you're feeling fancy. Wash it down with an ice cold (if the cooler was working) Pabst Blue Ribbon beer.

It sounds so simple, so easy, but like Nashville itself, the key is this: you have to be there to fully appreciate it. The tastes, the smells, and the sounds. You had to be there on that New Year's Day when the city woke up, like a sleeping giant with a craving for fried bologna, and the slow day that had been predicted turned into a tidal wave of humanity that flooded both floors of Robert's. A first-time cook and a veteran bartender rode out the storm for five and a half hours, with only each other to lean on. No door guys. No barback. No servers. Don't ask me how it happened. I only know that it did.

Before my time at Robert's was over, I had worked every position available. I led the band, loosened clogged pipes, emptied the garbage, threw out the trash, cut the lemons and limes, and even carried the banner with my own radio program—and I loved doing it. Nashville is a transient town, though. People come and go, as quietly as the last of the faithful servants folding up the table tents and disappearing down the Ryman alley into the dawn.

Back in Warsaw, the candle is nearly burned out and the water has turned cold, but not to worry: "I'll never be blue, my dreams come true."

BLUE AFTERNOON

1½ ounces Reposado tequila

½ ounce orange juice

½ ounce lime juice

½ ounce blue curaçao (Giffard probably works best here)

1 can Pabst Blue Ribbon beer

Add the tequila, orange juice, lime juice, and blue curaçao to a pint glass over ice. Stir briskly, then top with the beer. Listen closely for a yearning pedal steel in the background.

MAYA BAY
p. 160

AUTOMA **SUPERSON**
p. 164

ZICATELA
p. 207

HARBOR LIGHT
p. 150-1

TEN

THE DRINKS FROM THE PROS

Think of these drinks as one long-form cocktail menu from a prolonged pandemic of living in a time warp. Taken together they offer plenty of creative inspiration and at-home hacks for making better drinks. →

THE FALL MINT JULEP

MIKE WOLF

With the Kentucky Derby pushed back to September 5 in 2020—the first time the race has been moved since 1945—I thought it was time to get creative with this late-spring staple, adding a mild autumnal twist to prepare for the colder evenings to come. Usually, my seasonal take on the Mint Julep involves the first of the summer blueberries, some late season flowering watercress, and the wildly fragrant young chocolate mint in my garden. For this riff on a classic, I'm playing some fall spices off the buttery, caramel-like goodness of Madeira, mixed with maple syrup, meant to conjure a crisp fall morning of waffles and coffee. Making a julep can seem like an overwhelming proposition for the home bartender, but think of this as an elaborately presented, luxurious Old-fashioned. Just don't forget the crushed ice.

   8 fresh mint leaves

   2 dashes Angostura bitters

   1 teaspoon maple syrup

   2 ounces Belle Meade bourbon

   1 teaspoon Rainwater Madeira

   Dash of cinnamon

   3 sprigs of fresh mint and a marigold flower, for garnish

In a mixing glass, add the mint leaves, bitters, and maple syrup and stir ingredients together, taking care to lightly muddle the mint

leaves together with the bitters and syrup with the back of your spoon.

Fill the mixing glass with ice and add the bourbon and Madeira and stir briskly for 15 seconds. Let the mixture rest while you set up the julep cup.

In a julep cup (or whatever you're drinking this mighty concoction out of), fill halfway with crushed ice and add the dash of cinnamon, then add more ice to fill the cup ¾ of the way full.

Strain the drink over the crushed ice and garnish with the three sprigs of mint, brushing the mint over the outsides of the cup and over the top of the drink. Fill with more crushed ice and a marigold flower, if you dare.

THE HARBOR LIGHT

MIKE WOLF

The yearning, echo-drenched opening guitar lines of Elvis Presley's "Harbor Lights," played with the deft touch and tossed-off brilliance of Elvis's band staple James Burton, always have the ability to transport me to some distant hammock by the sea. It's the sound of a star-splashed sky stretched out over an ocean of longing, with Elvis wistfully hoping by the end, "Someday, harbor lights will bring you back to me." Though in his aching loneliness, he doesn't seem so sure that it's going to work out. I felt that same hopelessness throughout the pandemic, wanting to get back home to see family, meet friends out for dinner, and one day, be able to make drinks for complete strangers again, connecting over the simple joy of the cocktail. This drink is inspired by the Port Light cocktail, excavated from obscurity by Jeff "Beachbum" Berry, author of Sippin' Safari and creator of the excellent Total Tiki app, which essentially puts the entire tiki drink canon in your pocket. The Port Light has always fascinated me, both for the beautiful red and gold tumbler made by Trader Vic to serve it in, and the fact that it was concocted in the tropical drinks haven of, uh ... Columbus, Ohio. The drink is credited to Sandro Conti, who tended bar at the Kahiki Supper Club in Columbus. One of the only classic tiki drinks to feature bourbon, it is also a study in flavor affinity, with the spice of the bourbon playing off the fruity tropicality of passionfruit, the lemon bridging the tart cheek-squeeze of passionfruit while also taming the sweetness in the syrup. For this riff on the Port Light, I've added an egg white and some Amaro Averna, making for a silky-smooth sipper to drift the night away. Someday, we'll be together again. With this in my hand, maybe I'm not in such a hurry after all.

2 ounces Old Soul bourbon

¾ ounce fresh lemon juice

½ ounce passionfruit cordial*

1 egg white (save the yolk for folding into your next pasta dish)

¼ ounce Amaro Averna

Tiniest pinch of Maldon sea salt

Mint or clover, for garnish

Add all ingredients except the garnish to a blender and pulse without ice for 20 seconds, which whips the egg white into the cocktail without breaking down the structure of the drink (which water will do). Add crushed ice to the blender and blend at a high speed for 8 seconds. Pour everything into your Port Light glass or tumbler and garnish with mint or flowering clover. Put on an Elvis record.

*TO MAKE THE PASSIONFRUIT CORDIAL:

8 ounces passionfruit puree

8 ounces simple syrup

Whisk the passionfruit puree into the simple syrup. Another way to add passionfruit flavor to your cocktails without breaking the bank is to use Republic of Tea's Passionfruit Papaya tea bags, steeping a few bags into a syrup. This passionfruit cordial will keep for a few weeks in the refrigerator.

THE GREEN VACCINE

KENNETH DEDMON :: CO-HOST, LIQUID GOLD PODCAST,
HUSK NASHVILLE BARTENDER

   1¼ ounces Bluecoat gin

   1 ounce fresh wheatgrass juice

   ¾ ounce fresh lemon juice

   Scant ½ ounce agave nectar

   1 barspoon Fernet-Branca

   2 mint leaves

   Cayenne powder, for garnish

Shake all ingredients except the garnish and strain into a chilled
rocks glass (neat). Garnish with a light dust of cayenne powder.

SPIEGELAUDER

SCOTT SOIFER :: FOLK, NASHVILLE, TN

1¼ ounces Fidencio mezcal

¾ ounce Cappelletti aperitivo

¾ ounce lime juice

¾ ounce grapefruit juice

¾ ounce simple syrup

1 can Bearded Iris Homestyle IPA

1 grapefruit peel, for garnish

Shake the mezcal, aperitivo, lime juice, grapefruit juice, and simple syrup and strain into a spiegelau (or other large beer) glass. Top with the IPA and garnish with a grapefruit peel, expressing the oils over the top of the glass and inserting the peel into the drink.

THE CIVIL SERVICE

PAT HALLORAN :: BAR MANAGER, HENRIETTA RED, NASHVILLE

  2 ounces dry gin

  ¾ ounce lemon juice

  ½ ounce honey

  ½ ounce orgeat syrup

Shake ingredients thoroughly until chilled and strain into a coupe glass. Garnish with a turn of a black pepper grinder. If you don't have a grinder, sprinkle some ground black pepper on top.

TRASHMOPOLITAN

FREDDY SCHWENK :: PARTNER, BAR ALLIANCE –
BAR/RESTAURANT ENTREPRENEUR

This is a "closed loop" Cosmopolitan variation, using husks from juiced citrus and berries and fruit that were already used to make a syrup previously. The "flavor" of the syrup will change based on what we have left over from prep.

> 1 ounce WÓDKA Vodka
>
> 1 ounce Control C Pisco
>
> ¾ ounce "trash syrup"
>
> ¾ ounce lime juice

Shake all the ingredients together and serve up in a cocktail glass or coupe.

nUMBER ONE

SHANNON WRIGHT :: BAR MANAGER, TWO TEN JACK

> **2 ounces Roku gin**
>
> **1 ounce Zucca rhubarb amaro**
>
> **1 ounce tamarind juice**
>
> **½ ounce passionfruit syrup**
>
> **¼ ounce lemon juice**
>
> **1 mint sprig, for garnish**
>
> **Splash of club soda (optional)**

Shake all ingredients except the garnish and club soda and serve on the rocks, garnishing with a mint sprig. Because we serve it on tap, there is a bit of effervescence in ours, so feel free to add a little soda.

THIEF'S ALIBI

BRANDON ANAMIER :: BAR MANAGER, SUNDAY VINYL, DENVER

> 1½ ounces Wheatley vodka
>
> 1 ounce golden milk coconut cream*
>
> ½ ounce egg white
>
> ½ ounce lemon juice
>
> ¼ ounce Vecchio Amaro del Capo

Build all ingredients in a tin and dry shake (without ice). Add ice and shake. Double strain and serve in a coupe. Garnish with black pepper.

*You can make your own golden milk spice blend, or like I did, buy a premixed version from my favorite local spice shop here in Denver. I combined one can of Coco Lopez Real Cream of Coconut with the golden milk powder (turmeric, cinnamon, clove) in a blender. Transfer into a squeeze bottle, and you have golden milk coconut cream.

GOLDEN HOUR

KELLY GABLE :: BAR MANAGER, JOSEPHINE

During quarantine I never stopped thinking about work; it was hard not to. We all had no idea if and when this thing would end. I have a fear of being unprepared, so every day I wanted to make sure I had drinks ready to go for a new menu when we reopened. Another thing I kept thinking about was those who have always supported me in my management journey at Josephine, and Standard Proof Whiskey Co. were always by my side. They even donated their whiskey to a fundraiser for tornado relief and matched the donation we made in sales. They're always ready to do more and help people, so I continuously experimented with their products. So, work, plus companies that mean something to me, helped me come up with this cocktail named Golden Hour. At Josephine, we mill our own sweet corn, similar to Cope's Dried Sweet Corn. We cook sweet corn down in dairy and herbs, dehydrate it, and use it for our menu items, such as the cornbread. I decided to take the dehydrated corn we have scattered all over the restaurant, rehydrate it, and add demerara sugar to the water I pulled. I added some Hickory Pecan Rye by Standard Proof, a heavy hand of Angostura, and I added a dash of Cocchi Vermouth di Torino for more body.

¾ ounce Copes Demerara syrup*

¼ ounce Cocchi Vermouth di Torino

4–5 dashes Angostura bitters

2 ounces Standard Proof Hickory Rye Pecan

Stir all the ingredients together, and strain over a large ice cube. No garnish is necessary.

*TO MAKE THE SYRUP:

1 pint dried corn

2 pints water

1 cup demerara sugar

Heat dried corn in the water until the water cooks down to 1 pint. Add the sugar.

APERITIF BELIEF

ALI BESTEN :: CATHEAD DISTILLERY

I have found that I love making wine and aperitif cocktails. Here is one that I have been enjoying in particular.

1 ounce Cathead honeysuckle vodka

1 ounce Cappelletti aperitivo

4 ounces Mountain Valley Sparkling Water, in Original or White Peach, or dry sparkling wine.

Mix together the vodka and Cappelletti. Top with sparkling water (or wine).

MAYA BAY

JAMIE WHITE :: CO-OWNER, PEARL DIVER AND LUCKY'S 3 STAR

This drink is called Maya Bay, and it is one of my favorites that I came up with after going to Thailand. These flavors together made me so happy. This is what I've been drinking at home during quarantine because it reminded me of great times.

- **2 ounces tequila**
- **1½ ounces mango curry mix***
- **¾ ounce lime juice**
- **2–3 ounces ginger beer**
- **Pinch red curry (to rim the glass)**
- **Pinch salt (to rim the glass)**

Shake the tequila, mango curry mix, and lime juice together. Top with ginger beer. Use the red curry and salt mixture to coat the rim of the glass.

*TO MAKE THE MANGO CURRY MIX:

- **1 ounce mango puree**
- **¾ ounce agave syrup**
- **1 barspoon of red curry**

In a small saucepan, add all ingredients and heat for 5 minutes. Bottle once cooled and refrigerate for up to two weeks.

QUEEN OF THE RODEO

DEMI NATOLI :: WHITE LIMOZEEN

Quarantine SUCKS. The week things shut down, we were getting ready to open White Limozeen. The week we were all so excited to open this brand-new bar, I had to lay off every single person on my staff. It was a really devastating time to have no answers for your staff on how to make money, how to pay their bills, how to keep them safe.

This cocktail is a riff on a Daiquiri Number 5 and a Hemingway Daiquiri, called a Daiquiri Crusta Especial. I knew if I put this on my menu with rum, it would not get ordered as much, so I made it with vodka, with the hope that I could persuade someone else to drink one of my favorites.

> **2 ounces vodka**
>
> **¾ ounce lime juice**
>
> **¾ ounce grapefruit juice**
>
> **½ ounce pomegranate syrup (or grenadine)**
>
> **¼ ounce Luxardo Maraschino liqueur**
>
> **Cowboy Dust (edible glitter and sugar mix), for garnish**

Shake all liquid ingredients together and strain into a coupe. Garnish with Cowboy Dust.

DRO'S TOM KAH

NICK DROHAN :: LEAD BARTENDER, CHOPPER

- **1 ounce rhum agricole**
- **1 ounce gold Jamaican rum**
- **¾ ounce flavor town cordial***
- **¾ ounce orange juice**
- **½ ounce lime juice**
- **½ ounce cream sherry**
- **½ ounce heavy coconut cream**
- **Pinch gold dust (MSG)**
- **Pinch of salt**
- **2 dashes Angostura bitters**
- **2–3 dashes Thai chili tincture (optional)**
- **1 mint sprig, 1 sprig cilantro, half wheel lime, and orange wheel, for garnish**

Shake all ingredients together with 4–5 large ice cubes. Open pour the drink into your favorite tiki mug and add crushed ice to fill. Garnish with mint, cilantro, lime, and orange wheel.

*TO MAKE THE FLAVOR TOWN CORDIAL:

- **2 cups sugar**
- **1 cup water**
- **4–5 coins ginger, peeled**

2 tablespoons turmeric, chopped (or 1 tablespoon dried)

¼ cup chopped lemongrass (or 2 tablespoons dried)

1 teaspoon paprika

2–3 ounces coconut water

Heat sugar and water and stir until sugar has dissolved. Then add the ginger, turmeric, lemongrass, and paprika and turn the heat up to a simmer. Let ingredients simmer, uncovered, for 20 minutes. Remove from heat to cool. Add coconut water to taste once the syrup has completely cooled.

OTRO VEZ

ALEXIS SOLER :: OWNER/OPERATOR NO. 308, OLD GLORY, FLAMINGO COCKTAIL CLUB, AND FALCON COFFEE BAR

1½ ounces mezcal

¾ ounce carrot juice

¼ ounce fresh orange juice

¾ ounce coconut crème (such as Coco Lopez)

¼ ounce lime juice

Pinch of salt

Shake all ingredients together and strain into Collins glass over fresh ice.

AUTOMATIC SUPERSONIC HYPNOTIC FUNKY FRESH

SALLY GATZA :: BAR MANAGER, LA JACKSON

This is just a simple, vegetal, slightly savory Mezcal Mule that should be pretty easy to make at home.

- 1½ ounces mezcal
- ¾ ounce ginger syrup
- ¾ ounce lime juice
- ¾ ounce green bell pepper juice
- ¼ ounce Ancho Reyes Verde liqueur
- 1 nasturtium leaf or other flower, for garnish

Shake all liquid ingredients together and strain into a glass. Garnish with a nasturtium leaf, flower, or whatever you have on hand!

"WHAT DAY IS IT?"

DEVIN DRAKE :: BAR MANAGER,
REDHEADED STRANGER

*After being furloughed with a completely diminished home bar,
I decided to run out and buy bottles of gin and tequila. I really
didn't have much intent to make cocktails with them; I just wanted
to drink them on the rocks or with a splash of soda. You know,
keeping it easy because, well, quarantine. However, later that
evening I had the cocktail itch with very few ingredients on hand. I
pulled stuff I had and basically came up with an easy "drink for the
people at home" that most everyone has the ingredients for.*

> 2 ounces Sipsmith Gin
>
> 1 ounce fresh lemon juice
>
> ¾ ounce maple syrup
>
> 1 egg white
>
> 2–3 dashes Angostura bitters

In shaker combine gin, lemon juice, syrup, and egg white. Dry shake
for 30 seconds.

Add ice and shake again. Serve up in whatever fancy glass you may
have (or drink it out of a coffee mug if you want—it's a pandemic!).
Top with a few dashes of Angostura bitters.

East Nashville SP'20

Zoning Out
Another Long Afternoon
Nothing For Me to Do.
I'm Killing Some Time, Killing Time Still
Over and Over
Day After Day - - -
After Fucking Day After Day...
It's Easy, They Say. I sat back and stare)
It was oddly peaceful. Some days.
I waited and waited. Rolled myself a J...
And waited some more
I think it's Thursday... Later in the month
So, — Another Long Afternoon
Begin Again → And Begin Again so
Everything well be Different
Hey,.. Are you There?

* Check out Patrick's playlist curated for this book project on Spotify called "Disintegration," by Patrick Wayne de Selector. I'm serious.

LITTLE MARLE

PATRICK GOODSPEED* :: PLAYLIST PROFESSIONAL AND
BARTENDER, NASHVILLE

1½ ounces mezcal (Del Maguey or something bold)

¾ ounce lime juice

½ ounce grapefruit juice

½ ounce rosemary simple syrup or agave syrup*

½ ounce Aperol

¼ ounce Cynar

2 dashes Angostura bitters

2 dashes Regan's Orange Bitters

**1 sprig of rosemary, grapefruit peel, or rosemary salt on
the rim of the glass, for the garnish**

Shake all the ingredients and strain into a coupe. Add garnish of your
choice.

*TO MAKE THE ROSEMARY SIMPLE SYRUP:

1 cup fresh rosemary

2 cups water

2 cups sugar

In a saucepan, slowly simmer the rosemary, water, and sugar for 20
minutes, until it is cooked down into a syrup. Remove from heat.
When completely cool, strain and bottle. It will keep for one month
in the refrigerator.

THE ONLY WAY TO SAY FAREWELL

ADAM SLOAN :: @SOUNDTRACKMYDRINK INSTAGRAM COCKTAIL PAGE

This cocktail is very special to me. I wanted to make a drink that my wife and I could both enjoy. So I started combining her favorite ingredients with mine: gins, vermouths, and amaro. I workshopped the specs with our friend, Albree Sexton, a bartender who lost her life in the March 3rd, 2020 tornado. So once I was satisfied with the ratios, I named it after a line from Once Upon A Time In Hollywood in order to say goodbye to Albree: "The Only Way To Say Farewell."

I've also been exploring music that, in my opinion, pairs nicely with this cocktail. So far, my absolute favorite is a song by LCD Soundsystem called "Dance Yrself Clean"—the lyrics are a perfect expression of how much I miss my favorite bars, my favorite bartenders, and my favorite memories.

*"I miss the way the night comes
With friends who always make it feel good
This basement has a cold glow
Though it's better than a bunch of others"*

> 1½ ounces gin (1 ounce Aviation gin, ½ ounce Drumshanbo gin)
>
> ¾ ounce Carpano Antica Formula vermouth
>
> ½ ounce Cynar 70

¼ ounce Amaro Montenegro

2 dashes orange bitters

Tiny splash of white balsamic vinegar (optional)

3 Castelvetrano olives, for the garnish

Stir all the liquid ingredients and serve over ice in a rocks glass. Garnish with the 3 olives on a skewer.

SHELTER COVE

RILEY PERRIN ELLIS :: ATTABOY (CREATED BY MIKE DOLFINI)

This was my favorite drink Mike made at Attaboy. It embodied him. Two of his favorite things: rum and scotch. Bitter, fruity, sweet, and smoky. For many of us, he was our comfort and our shelter. He was our best friend. I hope many people can enjoy this drink, share it with others, and think of him when they do.

1½ ounces Hamilton Pot Still Gold rum

½ ounce Laphroaig 10-Year-Old scotch

½ ounce Giffard Banane du Brésil

¼ ounce Amargo Vallet Amaro

1 orange peel, for garnish

Build liquid ingredients in double rocks glass over big ice, and garnish with an orange twist.

CHAMOMILE COOLER

LEAH SMITH :: BAR MANAGER, ETCH

I started making this right after the quarantine began, with the ingredients I had in the kitchen. I almost always have Sleepytime tea to drink before bedtime, but any kind of chamomile will have the same soothing effects. Chamomile is an herb used since ancient times to relax and soothe stressed nerves and anxious minds.

For the white wine, a dry riesling, sauvignon blanc, or pinot grigio will all work. I used a Vermentino because it was what was in my fridge when everything happened. Often when I have a bottle of wine, I end up with just a bit left in the bottle, not enough to have with a meal, but good for little additions to recipes.

I garnish this one with dandelion fluff because it's easy to find, in every yard, and dandelions are completely edible. There's also something very soothing and dreamy to the action of blowing the dandelion puff over your drink and letting a few little parasols float down to the surface of the drink. They are almost imperceptible to the tongue, as they are so delicate, but you can also just let them stick to the glass as you drink.

1½ ounces vodka

1 ounce strong brewed chamomile tea

½ ounce simple syrup

¼ ounce white wine

1 dandelion puff, for the garnish

Shake all liquid ingredients together with ice and strain into a small footed glass. Garnish with the dandelion puff.

FRAPPÉ-STYLE DAIQUIRI

ADRIENNE D. STONER :: FORMER LOST LAKE BARTENDER AND CURRENT MAISON FERRAND ON-PREMISE MANAGER

This drink was a fun Frappé-Style Daiquiri I put together. It's bittersweet, much like my time spent during the pandemic. The rum has changed a few times depending on what's in my house.

1 ounce Angostura bitters

1½ ounces coconut cream

¾ ounce Plantation Xaymaca rum

¾ ounce lime juice

½ tablespoon raw turbinado sugar

1½ cups crushed ice

1 fresh mint sprig and a lime wheel, for the garnish

Blend all ingredients except the garnish in a blender until cold. Serve in a large coupe glass or any glass fit for paradise. Garnish with mint and a lime wheel.

SPRUCE TIP GIMLET

NATHANIEL SMITH :: BAR DIRECTOR, TRAVAIL KITCHEN
AND PIG ATE MY PIZZA, MINNEAPOLIS

Spruce tips have a special place in northern climate cuisine. Not only is it one of the rare goods that has its own vitamin C, but the emergence of the bright green tips on conifer trees is the surefire sign that winter has truly left. Easily gathered and utilized by bartenders and chefs as well as amateur foragers, spruce tips are cheap, flavorful, and nondamaging to the trees if harvested correctly. Never overharvest from a single tree or area (a handful per tree is enough), attempt to harvest from the highest points you are able (many animals eat the buds on the lower branches), and most importantly, never harvest the center point of the three-pronged growth from each branch—doing so will stunt the growth of that branch. Simply run under cold water before use, and they are ready to consume, freeze, or infuse in honey, vinegar, spirits, bitters, or virtually anything needing a piney, spring flavor.

Why a Gimlet? Because it is simple and elegant, refreshing and balanced, and allows the fresh, woodsy flavors of the spruce tips to play uninterrupted with the juniper of the gin.

> **2 ounces of your favorite gin (juniper-forward, London Dry is recommended, although many spirits work as a substitute, from vodka to aquavit to unaged tequila)**
>
> **¾ ounce fresh lime juice (just squeezed and strained—nothing bottled)**
>
> **¾ ounce spruce tip cordial***
>
> **2 dashes orange bitters**

1 lime wheel and remaining spruce tip, for the garnish

Combine all ingredients except the garnish in a shaking tin and give a vigorous shake. Strain into chilled cocktail glass or over ice based on preference. Garnish with lime wheel and a remaining spruce tip.

*TO MAKE THE SPRUCE TIP CORDIAL:

4 cups water

4 cups fresh or frozen spruce tips

4 cups lime juice

8 cups white sugar

2 tablespoons coriander

1 large pinch salt

12 lime peels

1 orange peel

4–5 coins of fresh, peeled ginger

Combine water and spruce tips into a saucepan and bring to a boil. Turn down heat to low and simmer for 5 minutes. Once cooled, place into a jar and allow to sit overnight at room temperature.

The following day, blend the spruce tip water in a blender for ten seconds. Add all ingredients together in a large saucepan at this point and bring to a boil, simmering again for 5 minutes. Cool, strain into a clean vessel, and keep refrigerated. Because of the high acid and sugar content, this cordial will last a month, or can be frozen.

TEMPEST OF TANSY

ADAM MORGAN :: HEAD BARTENDER, HUSK, NASHVILLE

This spring has been a season of loss, transition, and growth for many of us. It's been a storm inside of a storm. This drink represents a period of transition and rejuvenation. I happened to be going through a big move as the initial wave of COVID-19 hit Tennessee. One of the last things I took with me before pulling out of my former house was a handful of tansy that had been planted the season before. Admittedly, I had neglected the garden this year and barely looked at it. So it came as a great surprise that the tansy bush was thriving and nearly as tall as me. I had to do something with it. In his tenure at Husk, Mike Wolf shared many words of wisdom with me. One was the usefulness of tansy, a fragrant and piney herb, in whiskey cocktails. I decided to swap out the whiskey for Castle & Key Restoration Gin. This gin's strong backbone, with its 106 proof and sharp, peppery, and herbaceous notes, was the perfect substitute.

> 2 ounces Castle & Key Restoration gin
>
> ¾ ounce lime juice
>
> ¾ ounce tansy shrub syrup*
>
> 2 dashes cardamom bitters
>
> 3 strawberry slices (muddled)
>
> Dried or fresh tansy, for the garnish

Combine all ingredients except the garnish into shaker tin. Fill with ice and shake. Double strain into a rocks glass with fresh ice. Garnish with dried or fresh tansy.

Fresh tansy leaves

2 cups hot water

2 cups sugar

¾ ounce apple cider vinegar

Steep the tansy leaves in the hot water for 3–5 minutes. Strain out tansy and whisk in sugar and apple cider vinegar. Refrigerate for 2–3 days before use. Keeps for up to two weeks.

CATAVINO

BRANDON BRAMHALL :: ATTABOY

2 dashes Angostura bitters

2 dashes orange bitters

1½ ounces Amontillado sherry

1½ ounces blanc vermouth

1 grapefruit peel, for garnish

Build liquid ingredients in a rocks glass, preferably frozen. Add ice (preferably large format) and stir 3–5 times. Garnish with a grapefruit peel.

PEAS EXCUSE ME

BRAD LANGDON :: BAR MANAGER, THE DABNEY CELLAR AND BAR, WASHINGTON, DC

2 ounces The Real McCoy 3-Year White Blended rum

1¼ ounces sugar snap pea cordial*

¾ ounce lime juice

2–3 dashes saline solution

Mint bouquet and cracked black pepper, for the garnish

Add all ingredients except for the garnish into a cocktail shaker. Add ice and shake. Strain out over crushed ice in a Collins glass. Add garnish.

*TO MAKE THE SUGAR SNAP PEA CORDIAL:

Sugar

Hot water

5 grams fresh mint

Fresh sugar snap pea juice

First, make a mint simple syrup by combining a 1:1 sugar to hot water ratio. Steep the mint in the mixture for about an hour. Then, add the pea juice to the syrup in a 2:1 ratio.

SAKE AND SPICE

MATT BURNETT :: BAR MANAGER, PM RESTAURANT, NASHVILLE

I created this cocktail at the request of the Head Chef/Co-Owner of PM, Arnold Myint. Arnold asked me to create a cocktail for the event "Taste," which is a fundraising event for the LGBTQ community in Nashville with an emphasis on LGBTQ business owners. The event incorporated many restaurants and businesses from Nashville and included different judged categories, such as best appetizer, best dessert, best entree, and best cocktail. I was humbled to win the best cocktail category, and honestly was just happy to be part of a meaningful exhibition of what Nashville has to offer. The cocktail, named "Sake and Spice," is as follows.

1 ounce Proper Sake Co.'s The Diplomat Junmai sake

¾ ounce Tanqueray No. Ten gin

½ ounce fresh squeezed lemon juice

½ ounce cranberry juice

½ ounce simple syrup

1 dash Bar Keep Apple bitters

Shake all ingredients with ice until chilled and serve in whichever glass you prefer. No garnish necessary.

YELLOW EYES

TARYN BREEN :: NASHVILLE

This original cocktail takes its cue from the classic "French 75." The name is also one of my favorite songs by local Nashville musician Rayland Baxter, making this the perfect drink and tunes combo for a lazy spring day in a very quiet Music City.

FOR THE COCKTAIL:

- ¾ ounce fresh lemon juice
- ½ ounce rosemary syrup*
- ½ ounce Golden Moon Ex Gratia Génépi (Yellow Chartreuse or other Génépi will work as well)
- 1½–2 ounces gin of preference (I used Broker's London Dry)
- 1–2 ounces dry sparkling wine, such as cava, to top
- 1 lemon peel and rosemary sprig, for the garnish

Combine ingredients except the garnish and shake. Then double strain into a flute or a coupe glass, and top with dry sparkling wine. Garnish with lemon twist and rosemary sprig.

*TO MAKE THE ROSEMARY SYRUP:

- 1 cup sugar
- 1 cup water
- 10–12 sprigs of rosemary (leaves only)

Combine sugar and water and bring to a boil. Stir in rosemary leaves. Remove from heat, steep for 4–6 hours, and strain solids. You can also add a tablespoon of high-proof neutral grain spirit (I used 100 proof vodka). This will keep your syrup for up to three months.

BOOZY BANANA BREAD

KYNSEY HUNTER :: BAR MANAGER, LOCUST

A quarantine cocktail I kept trying—while everyone was making banana bread or sourdough—was to attempt a "cocktail version" of those things. I am NOT a baker. This drink has ripe banana, pecan, and a yeasty umami kick at the end.

   ¾ ounce high-proof whiskey

   ½ ounce Giffard Banane du Brésil

   ½ ounce Rivulet Pecan liqueur

   2 ounces Proper Sake Co. Super Gold Sparkling sake

Shake the whiskey, Banane du Brésil, and pecan liqueur together, and serve up in a coupe. Top with Proper Sake Super Gold Sparkling sake.

EPISODE 2: THE BREAKFAST FIZZ

MERCEDES O'BRIEN :: BAR MANAGER, COLD BEER, ATLANTA

- ½ teaspoon whole milk plain yogurt
- ½ teaspoon apple cider vinegar
- ¼ ounce lemon juice
- ½ ounce grapefruit juice
- 1 ounce strawberry tops syrup*
- 1½ ounces London dry gin
- 1 ounce soda water
- 1 sprig of basil, for garnish

Add all ingredients except soda water and basil into tin, with ice, and shake until well chilled. Add soda water and toss to combine. Double strain into rocks glass over ice. Garnish with basil.

*TO MAKE THE STRAWBERRY TOPS SYRUP:

- 1 cup strawberry tops
- 1 cup sugar
- 1 cup water
- ¼ teaspoon vanilla extract

Fashion a double boiler using a small pot with a few inches of water in it and topping with a heat-safe bowl. Add all ingredients into bowl, stirring ingredients to combine, and cover with plastic wrap.

Add double boiler to stove and cook under a medium-low to low flame for 30 minutes, or until tops become pale or translucent. Strain through a fine mesh strainer and allow to cool. Store in a food safe container in the refrigerator for up to two weeks.

MUTUALLY ASSURED DESTRUCTION

NICK THAXTON :: GENERAL MANAGER, CHOPPER

2 inches of cucumber peel, diced

6–8 mint leaves

½ ounce honey syrup

¾ ounce lime juice

½ ounce Green Chartreuse liqueur

¾ ounce Neisson Rhum Agricole Blanc

¾ ounce Wray & Nephew rum

Cucumber slices and mint sprigs, for garnish

Muddle the diced cucumber peel and mint leaves. Add the honey, lime juice, Green Chartreuse, Agricole Rhum, and Wray & Nephew rum. Swirl around in shaker tin, strain, and then shake with ice and strain into a coupe. Garnish with cucumber slices and a mint sprig.

HAPPENSTANCE

ERIN BARNETT :: FOUNDER, SPIRIT ANIMAL CO OPERATIVE, NASHVILLE

The cocktail came about because I made (and drank) one fresh and delicious cocktail that reminded me of an Italian grandfather–style drink (nod to Jessica Backhus), and I needed more booze in my evening when I learned that Davidson County would be on lockdown for an indeterminate amount of time due to COVID-19. At the time, I was looking at homeschooling my brilliant 9-year-old and trying to figure out how to keep my business afloat in a market that was just devastated by a tornado and then, two weeks later, being put on pause because of a virus that had affected the world. More booze was needed. These are some products that are amazing and new and not super well-known across Nashville, so I love bringing things like them to light.

> 2 ounces Western Grace brandy
>
> 1 ounce Casa D'Aristi Kalani Coconut liqueur
>
> 1 ounce Padró & Co. Rojo Amargo vermouth
>
> 1 ounce citrus simple syrup*
>
> 1 citrus peel, for garnish

Build the liquid ingredients in a rocks glass over ice and garnish with a citrus peel (whatever you have on hand).

*TO MAKE THE CITRUS SIMPLE SYRUP:

> 1 lemon, zested

1 orange, zested

1 cup of water

1 cup of sugar

In a small saucepan, add the lemon and orange zest to the water and sugar. Simmer for 15 minutes. Let the syrup completely cool on the stove top, then strain, bottle, and keep in the refrigerator for two weeks.

THE GOOD SAMARITAN

PAUL ROGERS :: HEAD BARTENDER, THE MARSH HOUSE, NASHVILLE

1 ounce bourbon (I like a nice mellow corn-blaster like Buffalo Trace)

1 ounce Amontillado sherry

1 ounce Giffard Banane du Brésil

1 ounce lemon juice

1 dehydrated lemon wheel, for garnish

Shake up all ingredients except the garnish and strain it over a large block of ice. Garnish with the lemon wheel.

GOOD AS GOLD

ALICIA SWARTZ :: NASHVILLE

I first made shrubs (sipping vinegars) at my last job as beverage director. During quarantine, I started making my shrubs, at home with fruits and vegetables that needed to get used. I started with a strawberry, serrano pepper, and lime shrub, then a date, fig, and rosemary one. I then became more adventurous with the sweetener and vinegar choices. I started using mainly turbinado sugar, and then cutting the white vinegar (because vinegars aren't cheap) with champagne vinegar, white wine vinegar, white balsamic vinegar, rice vinegar, and so on. I will continue to experiment with the sweetener options to lessen the amount of refined sugars going forward.

My recipe, as of now, is an equal ratio, 1:1:1, of the mixed edible part (fruit, vegetables, herbs, spices), sugar (or sweetener), and vinegar of choice. I combine the food mix with the sweetener and let it macerate for 24 hours. Depending on the potency of the spice, I may add them later in the shrub-making. I then introduce vinegar to the mix and allow it to sit at room temperature for 5–7 days, stirring daily. At the end of this time, I triple strain out any and all food particles from the liquid. You may want to save the vinegar-soaked fruit or vegetables for other applications. Finally, you're left with a tart and sweet nectar to use in cocktails, mocktails, or even vinaigrettes.

The one I'm using in my quarantine cocktail is a corn and black pepper shrub. About two years ago my partner and I visited Henley for after-dinner drinks. I remember seeing "corn shrub" in

a drink on their cocktail menu. Unfortunately, they were out of the shrub, but that stuck with me, and ever since, I was left with a desire to create them. I had heard of shrubs before, but I had never thought of mixing vegetables into them. For these, I used fresh corn, cut the kernels off, and milked the cobs. I combined all of this with turbinado sugar and let it rest for 24 hours. I then introduced a combination of ½ white distilled vinegar and ½ white *wine vinegar and let it sit for 7 days. I then triple strained it and added black peppercorns in cheesecloth to sit in the shrubs for 4 days. It has a yeasty smell, a creamy mouthfeel because of the starches, and is buttery and sweet-tasting, with a bit of tang from the vinegars. It goes toe-to-toe with blueberry and lemon as my favorite shrub so far.*

> **1¾ ounces Espolòn Añejo (I tried it with the Repo too, really good as well)**
>
> **¾ ounce corn and black pepper shrub**
>
> **½ ounce Suze Gentian liqueur**
>
> **¼ ounce lemon juice**
>
> **Garnish***

Combine all ingredients except the garnish ingredients in shaker with ice. Shake well. Double strain into chilled and crusted (see garnish below) Nick and Nora glass.

*TO MAKE THE GARNISH:

> **1–2 tablespoons clarified butter (ghee)**
>
> **Salt and pepper**
>
> **1 lemon peel**
>
> **2 sprigs of lemon thyme**

Coat ⅓ of the rim of the glass in clarified butter, about ½ inch thick. Coat salt and pepper crust on the clarified butter, being careful not to get any on the inside of the glass. Peel and express a lemon peel over the top of the glass. Cut a slit in the lemon peel to hang a sprig of lemon thyme through it.

MR. SPARKLE

TRAVIS ALLEN ARCHER :: BAR MANAGER,
OSTERIA LA BUCA, LOS ANGELES

This was my favorite drink on the cocktail list at my job, Osteria La Buca in Los Angeles, CA. It has great backbone and is so much lighter than a whiskey-forward cocktail. The Verjus and aloe add some crispness and acidity, and the Yuzu liqueur has a great zing, but the combination of everything together was a very refreshing, light, crushable spirit-forward cocktail for those hot Southern California days.

The name comes from an episode of The Simpsons called "In Marge We Trust," where Homer thinks a Japanese conglomerate has stolen his likeness for a detergent called "Mr. Sparkle."

1½ ounces Yuzu Yuzuri liqueur

¾ ounce Suntory Toki Whisky

¼ ounce Chareau Aloe liqueur

¼ ounce Verjus Blanc

2 dashes Bitter Queen tobacco bitters

Black pepper, for garnish

Stir all ingredients except the garnish. Serve over a large ice cube with a crack of black pepper.

THE BOLD ADVENTURE

JESSICA BACKHUS :: LEAD BARTENDER, DELANEY OYSTER HOUSE, CHARLESTON, SOUTH CAROLINA

I am probably most known for making the "Italian Grandpa" style of cocktail—we call it that because if you had an Italian grandfather, you know that he would sit on his porch all day and sip on these light, refreshing, uncomplicated elixirs. It is also such an open category because there are really no rules, but this type of drink generally follows the guidelines that it: A) is easy to make; B) has only a few ingredients and is some combination of bitter, sweet, and effervescent; and C) makes you happy. I also love tiki drinks, and I really love making dynamic nonalcoholic drinks. The coffee cordial is a great base to make an energizing, unleaded beverage—I like to combine it with tonic water and zested orange and call it a day.

The Bold Adventure is all of my faves—Italian Grandpa, tiki cocktail, any-hour beverage—rolled into one. It's simple to execute, yet complex and delicious to enjoy. The drink is named after the ship of a legendary female pirate named Arabella Drummond, who was known to pillage and bury treasure throughout the Caribbean and coastal southeastern United States. It's also aptly named for the experience of enjoying the drink, and the unknown future we are all tumbling into. My suggested movie pairing for this cocktail is The Goonies.

1 ounce rum (I use El Dorado or Flor de Caña)

1 ounce Cocchi Americano aperitif

½ ounce coffee cocoa nib cordial*

¼ ounce lime juice

1 dash Angostura bitters or Bittermen Tiki bitters

2–3 ounces soda water

1 lime cheek, for garnish

Build liquid ingredients in a glass over ice. Jostle or stir. Squeeze skin side of lime cheek into glass, then drop it in skin side up, like an umbrella!

*TO MAKE THE COFFEE COCOA NIB CORDIAL:

1 cup coffee

½ cup cherry syrup or raw or brown sugar

2 tablespoons cocoa nibs

¹⁄₁₆ teaspoon citric acid

In a small saucepan, simmer all ingredients for 20 minutes. Allow to cool and steep overnight. Strain out cocoa nibs, seal, and refrigerate.

This is a great use for leftover coffee and for cherry syrup if you strain the syrup out of your cocktail cherries (so that you can steep them in brandy or whiskey, like a good cocktail nerd!). If you don't have cherry syrup, raw or brown sugar is delicious—brown will make the cordial richer in flavor.

TERRA FIRMA MIX

MATT TOCCO :: BEVERAGE DIRECTOR,
STRATEGIC HOSPITALITY

We have spent a good amount of time during this ordeal cleaning, organizing, and touching up paint at the Patterson House. Before heading home, we have been enjoying some of the opened products that would lose their peak flavor before we opened the bar back up. One of the favorites thus far has been our Terra Firma batch, with Sprite and sparkling wine. Terra Firma makes a great base for sours and bucks when operating a functioning bar with fresh juices and syrups ready to go.

TO MAKE A LARGE BATCH OF THE MIX:

> **1500 milliliters Pisco**
>
> **750 milliliters Luxardo Maraschino Liqueur**
>
> **500 milliliters Campari**
>
> **1 ounce Angostura Orange bitters**
>
> **1 pineapple, deskinned and chunked**

Combine ingredients and let sit overnight. Blend and strain into a container.

TO MAKE ONE DRINK:

Pour a liberal amount (2–3 ounces) of Terra Firma Mix into a glass with ice and top with 3 ounces Sprite and 4 ounces sparkling wine. It would probably be good with a squeeze of lime for garnish.

PANIC BUTTON

RYAN CASEY :: BEVERAGE DIRECTOR, THE LIVING ROOM BAR
AT THE DEWBERRY

> 1½ ounces bourbon (I recommend Four Roses Yellow Label)
>
> ¾ ounce Amaro Averna
>
> ½ ounce Campari
>
> ½ ounce Heering cherry liqueur
>
> ¼ ounce lemon juice
>
> 55 millimeter sphere of ice (or really big ice cube), optional
>
> 1 lemon peel, for garnish

Using ice tongs, place the ice in the center of a chilled coupe. Then, combine all ingredients except the garnish in a shaker tin and shake hard for 30 seconds. Strain through fine mesh strainer. Express lemon over the coupe and discard peel.

WISCONSIN APPLE PIE

CARLEY GASKIN :: HOSPITALITY 201, CHICAGO (WINNER OF THE BOMBAY SAPPHIRE MOST IMAGINATIVE BARTENDER 2019)

This drink was originally created for the Final Challenge for Most Imaginative Bartender and has since been tweaked to perfection. I often refer to my style of bartending as "strange and delicious," and this drink perfectly showcases just that.

1½ ounces Cheddar Cheese Fat Washed Bombay Sapphire

¼ ounce salted lime caramel

½ ounce lemon juice

1 ounce cold-pressed Granny Smith apple juice

2 dashes smoked sea salt saline

Shake all ingredients together and serve up.

COME OUT TONIGHT

JOSHUA "WOODY" WILLIS :: FOOD AND BEVERAGE DIRECTOR, 4TH AND PEABODY: A NASHVILLE TAVERN

The drinks that are getting me through this are shots with friends via the internet: Evan Williams BIB, Titos, chartreuse, Skrewball, fernet, and of course, Wild Turkey 101. If I'm looking for an actual cocktail though, I've been sipping on this low ABV joint I created for the last menu at 4th and Peabody. It's the perfect little sipper for those "sitting on the porch days," especially when it starts heating up outside.

> 1 ounce Lustau Sherry PX
>
> ½ ounce Giffard strawberry liqueur
>
> 2 dashes saline (or a small pinch of salt)
>
> 3–4 ounces Topo Chico
>
> 1 lemon peel and strawberry slice, for garnish

Build sherry, strawberry liqueur, and saline in a Collins glass. Stir, and fill with cracked ice. Top with Topo Chico. Garnish with lemon peel and strawberry slice.

ADRIANA

ANDY WEDGE :: MOMOFUKU BAR WAYO, NEW YORK CITY

1½ ounces blanco tequila (Cimarron Blanco)

½ ounce limoncello

½ ounce Contratto Bitter

½ ounce lemon juice

½ ounce hibiscus chili syrup*

1 lemon wheel, for garnish

Shake all ingredients together and double strain over large rock. Garnish the drink with the thinnest lemon wheel possible, resting on top of a large ice cube.

TO MAKE A NONALCOHOLIC VERSION OF THE COCKTAIL:

4 ounces iced tea (we use oolong)

1½ ounces hibiscus chili syrup*

¾ ounce lemon juice

1 lemon wedge, for garnish

Shake all ingredients together and pour into iced tea glass. Garnish with lemon wedge.

*TO MAKE THE HIBISCUS CHILI SYRUP:

30 grams dried hibiscus

7 grams red pepper flakes

1 quart simple syrup

Combine 1 cup sugar and 1 cup water in a saucepan to make simple syrup. Heat until sugar is dissolved, stirring to combine. Remove from heat.

After making simple syrup, while still hot, steep all ingredients at room temperature for 3½ hours. Strain and chill before using in the cocktail.

SAFE WORD

JEREMIAH JASON BLAKE :: LEAD BARTENDER, BASTION RESTAURANT

It's 2021—everybody should have one!
As a side note, this drink might have been inspired by a shot from Green Hour, called Danger Zone, and a deep affinity for Top Gun.

1½ ounces mezcal (I recommend Banhez)

¾ ounce lime juice

¾ ounce Green Chartreuse liqueur

¾ ounce blue curaçao (I recommend Giffard)

Lime twist or dehydrated lime wheel, for garnish

Shake all ingredients except the garnish and strain into a coupe. Garnish with a lime twist (or dehydrated lime wheel).

COMING UP ROSES

LAUREN FELDMAN :: VALLEY BAR AND BOTTLE, SONOMA, CA

Don't get me wrong. I'm drinking a lot of wine right now. My preference is bubbles—champagne ideally, but almost any will do—or Chablis. That much never really changes. What's different about my time at home in isolation, however, is my desire to take part in the things I'm making. I'm not a cocktail person. Even when I order a cocktail in a bar, I want it to be simple: mezcal with a little orange juice or an orange slice, an über-traditional martini with a twist or olives, tequila on the rocks. I just feel so idle right now. I'm in the process of opening my first restaurant with a few friends in Sonoma, CA, my hometown. I moved back here from Nashville in 2015 and have been looking for a space ever since. We took ownership of the restaurant, called Valley, facing the town's main square and city hall in October 2019. It's a historic old building with incredible old bones and spooky history. What we thought would be a quick turnaround has turned into a six-month construction affair, which got shut down in the middle of March because of COVID-19. We were caught in some sort of limbo, as restaurants are considered essential, but apparently the construction of one . . . not so much.

So, idle since the middle of March, I've turned to what most restaurant people do: cooking, baking, and creating. I've decided to put in this book a simple little creation that's easy to make but can easily change with whatever is blowing up in your garden or down your block on walks. A steeped syrup, this time made with roses from my garden. Simple syrup is the easiest thing to make— equal parts sugar and water heated on the stove until the sugar

melts. I like mine to be a little runny for additions into cocktails, so I go a little heavier on the water. Once heated, I add fistfuls of rose petals in different colors to the mixture, keep it hot for 10 minutes, and then just let it steep while cooling for another 10 minutes before straining. It creates such a happy color and smells so blissful.

For my cocktail of choice, I pour 2 ounces of something bitter (Amaro Averna, Campari, etc.—I've currently been enjoying Amaro

Angeleno, a citrusy, floral little number) with ½ ounce of rose syrup, dump in a bunch of ice cubes, top with club soda, and, if you're feeling frisky, some sparkling wine. We happened to make a pét-nat in our garage last fall with grapes from a friend's vineyard. While we're planning to pour it at our opening party, it makes me sad to look at it and not drink it right now, so that's been the perfect topper, with its vibrant fuchsia hue adding to the sunrise beauty of this drink. It's basically a spritz, just made a bit more personal and timely by adding bits of your own creation. I love you, Nashville.

> 2 ounces Amaro Angeleno (any kind of bitters will do)
>
> ½ ounce rose syrup*
>
> 2–3 ounces club soda
>
> *Or* 3–4 ounces sparkling wine

Combine bitters and syrup in a glass. Add ice cubes. Top with club soda or sparkling wine, if desired.

*TO MAKE THE ROSE SYRUP:

> 2 cups sugar
>
> 3 cups water
>
> 1 cup rose petals

In a saucepan, combine the sugar and water and heat over low heat until the sugar melts. Then add rose petals and keep hot for 10 minutes. Allow to cool for 10 minutes, and strain into a container. Covered and kept in the refrigerator, the syrup will keep for at least one month.

THE SPAGHETTI WESTERN

CRAIG SCHOEN :: CO-OWNER/BEVERAGE DIRECTOR, PENINSULA

This is a recipe that's great for any season!

- 1½ ounces rye
- ¾ ounce Campari
- ¼ ounce Spanish vermouth rojo
- ¼ ounce falernum liqueur
- 10 mint leaves
- 2–3 ounces ginger beer
- Lime wheel, for garnish

Shake rye, Campari, vermouth, falernum, and mint leaves together and strain into a Collins glass. Top with ginger beer and lime.

CLASSIC SPANISH VERMOUTH COCKTAIL

CRAIG SCHOEN :: CO-OWNER/BEVERAGE DIRECTOR, PENINSULA

This is another recipe with Spanish vermouth that works well as a spring cocktail.

2 ounces Spanish vermouth rojo (I like Vermut, P. Quiles, or Yzaguirre reserve)

2 barspoons of olive brine

4 dashes Regan's orange bitters

2 ounces soda

1 olive and orange wedge, for garnish

Build vermouth, olive brine, and bitters in a large wine glass or rocks glass. Top with soda and garnish with an olive and orange wedge.

HOT TADASHI

GRAHAM FUZE :: BUTCHERTOWN HALL AND TWO TEN JACK

This was a drink I used to make at Two Ten Jack, and I just loved it.

- 1½ ounces bourbon (or Japanese whiskey, for extra points)
- ¼ ounce demerara simple syrup
- ¼ ounce lemon juice
- 2 dashes aromatic bitters
- Strip of lemon peel, expressed
- 3 ounces hot sake

Preheat a mug. Then add the bourbon, simple syrup, lemon juice, and bitters. Express the lemon peel. Then add the hot sake. Drink and be warm!

DIAMOND CUTTER

BRICE HOFFMAN :: NO. 308, ROLF AND DAUGHTERS, URBAN COWBOY, AND WOODLAND WINE MERCHANT

As much as we are drinking at home right now, I wanted a low ABV option that was easy to make and light enough for the spring weather. I hate getting out all my tools, so this is a pretty easy build—but it has tons of complexity and a light bitterness that keeps you reaching for a second sip.

This drink was named after the signature move of WWE legend Diamond Dallas Page.

1 ounce Cocchi Americano

1 ounce Dolin dry vermouth

1 ounce Aurora Amontillado sherry

1 pump (full pipette) Bittermens Xocolatl Mole bitters

1 orange peel, for garnish

Stir liquid ingredients in mixing glass over ice and strain into a Nick and Nora glass. Garnish with an orange peel, expressed and discarded.

STANDARD PROOF WILDFLOWER LEMONADE

ROBERT LONGHURST :: CREATIVE DIRECTOR, STANDARD PROOF SPIRITS, NASHVILLE

2 ounces Standard Proof Wildflower Rye

¾ ounce lemon juice

¾ ounce simple syrup

Cold tap water

Shake and strain the rye, lemon juice, and simple syrup into a tall glass with ice. Top with cold water.

FOXY BROWN

LIZ ENDICOTT :: CO-OWNER, BEVERAGE DIRECTOR, LYRA

1½ ounces gin

1 ounce hibiscus tea*

½ ounce lemon juice

2 dashes of cardamom bitters

ginger beer

Add gin, hibiscus tea, lemon juice, and bitters to a tin and shake with ice. Strain into a Collins glass full of ice and top with ginger beer.

*TO MAKE THE HIBISCUS TEA:

1 quart of water

1 cup dried hibiscus flowers

½ cup sugar

Boil 1 quart water and remove from heat. Add dried hibiscus flowers and sugar, stir, and let steep for 20 minutes. Strain through a fine mesh strainer or a coffee filter, and refrigerate for up to five days.

THAT'S A PEACH HUN

EDDIE ADAMS :: JOSEPHINE AND THE OPTIMIST, NASHVILLE

1 ounce vin de pêche*

4 ounces prosecco

1 orange or lemon peel, for garnish

Fill wine glass with ice. Add vin de pêche. Top with prosecco. Express or insert citrus peel.

*TO MAKE THE VIN DE PÊCHE:

2 cinnamon sticks

Small handful of whole cloves

10 allspice berries

Approx. 80 peach tree leaves

1⅛ liters (approx. one and a half 750-milliliter bottles) of sweet red wine

½ cup Laird's apple brandy

½ cup sugar, heaping

Toast baking spices in a frying pan on low heat until fragrant. Let cool. Wash and pat dry the peach leaves. Toss the leaves and spice into jar. Pour the wine (I used Beaujolais Nouveau, but any sweet wine will do) and the brandy into jar. Pour in sugar and mix. Let sit in cool, dark place for 10–15 days. After it sits, strain and enjoy in a drink!

WE GOT THE JAZZ

CHRIS CAPALDI :: BEVERAGE DIRECTOR, MCCONNEL
HOSPITALITY GROUP, FRANKLIN, TN

2 ounces jasmine green tea–infused Cathead vodka*

½ ounce Domaine de Canton ginger liqueur

½ ounce citrus cordial**

1 lime wheel and mint leaf, for garnish

Combine ingredients into cocktail shaker with ice. Shake well and double strain through a fine mesh strainer into a prechilled coupe. Garnish with a lime wheel and mint leaf.

*TO MAKE THE JASMINE GREEN TEA–INFUSED CATHEAD VODKA:

1 liter of Cathead vodka

4 individual serving bags of jasmine green tea

Combine vodka and tea bags in container and allow to steep at room temperature for 2 hours. Remove tea bags and squeeze out remaining liquid. Rebottle the vodka.

**TO MAKE THE CITRUS CORDIAL—MORGENTHALER METHOD:

3¾ cups sugar

Zest or peels from 4 limes and 2 grapefruit

3 ounces lime juice

3 ounces grapefruit juice

2½ ounces citric acid by volume (jigger it)

24 ounces hot water

Combine all ingredients into a blender, adding hot water last. It doesn't need to be boiling; it could just be from the hot water spigot on your tea/coffee maker. Blend on high for 30 seconds. Allow blended mixture to sit for 10 minutes to cool. Strain through a fine mesh strainer lined with cheesecloth. It's important to use the cheesecloth to catch as much of the ground-up pulp and peel as possible. Put in a container with a lid and refrigerate for up to a month.

ZICATELA

GABE FUENMAYOR :: OWNER/PROPRIETOR, BAR SOVEREIGN, NASHVILLE

1½ ounces Mala Idea Mezcal Espadin

¾ ounce celery juice

¾ ounce Granny Smith apple juice

½ ounce lime juice

¼ ounce cinnamon demerara syrup

Shake all ingredients together and serve up in coupe or Nick and Nora glass.

MEADMOSA

DRU SOUSAN :: CO-OWNER, HONEYTREE MEADERY, NASHVILLE

This drink is made with Lil Batch, our light and floral, low-ABV signature mead.

> **2 ounces Honeytree Meadery "Lil Batch"**
>
> **3 ounces orange juice**
>
> **Prosecco to top**
>
> **Summer berries, for garnish**

Combine the mead and orange juice in a wine glass or flute. Top with prosecco (preferably) or another light sparkling wine. Garnish with any combination of summer berries (blueberries, strawberries, blackberries, or raspberries).

BOXED-IN SOUR

STEFANIE MARSHALL :: BARTENDER AND WRITER, LOS ANGELES

I realize this is a common "classic" cocktail most bartenders would know as a New York Sour. While it's always one that I like to order at a bar, it also happened to be one of the only cocktails I could make from what I had at home during the beginning of quarantine, when I couldn't leave my house for the ingredients for something more elaborate or fancy. Whenever I would post this beauty in my Instagram stories, I would get so many messages asking what it was that I sent "how to" videos to some people. It accidentally became my quarantine cocktail.

> **1½ ounces of whatever whiskey you have hanging around**
>
> **¾ ounce lemon juice**
>
> **½ ounce simple syrup**
>
> **1½ ounces boxed red wine (or bottled, if you're fancy!)**

In a shaker (or whatever you make cocktails in at home), add the whiskey, lemon juice, and simple syrup over ice. Shake vigorously, and then strain into a small glass over fresh ice. (You could also dump with shaken ice if ice is scarce in your house.)

For a layered cocktail effect, use the back side of a small spoon and pour the red wine slowly over the spoon into the whiskey concoction. If you don't care about aesthetics, just pour in the wine and stir.

CHARLIE'S OLD-FASHIONED #3

CHARLIE NELSON :: FOUNDER, NELSON'S GREEN BRIER DISTILLERY

Something that I love about whiskey is how it slows things down and brings people together. We are all humans, with more in common than we realize sometimes. Whiskey breaks down barriers and helps remind us of our shared humanity. When good whiskey is flowing, you'll never meet a stranger.

2 ounces Belle Meade bourbon

¼ ounce maple syrup

1 dash Angostura bitters

1 dash Peychaud's bitters

Orange peel, for garnish

Add all ingredients except the orange peel to a mixing glass with ice and stir briefly. Strain into a rocks glass over ice and garnish with an orange peel expressed over the drink.

OH HAL!

ROBERT JONES :: OWNER/OPERATOR, METEOR, MINNEAPOLIS

This drink was our top-selling cocktail at Meteor, my new bar I opened in late 2019, before we closed. We didn't have too much data to draw on, since we were only open for three months before the shutdown. We are now back open!

1 ounce Cynar

1 ounce mezcal

½ ounce simple syrup

¾ ounce fresh lime juice

3 mint leaves, torn

2 ounces ginger beer

1 mint sprig, for garnish

Combine all ingredients except garnish and shake hard. Strain into an ice-filled Collins glass and top with ginger beer. Garnish with a fresh spanked mint sprig.

ENDLESS SUMMER OLD-FASHIONED

LAURA UNTERBERG :: THE FOX BAR AND COCKTAIL CLUB, NASHVILLE

This Old-fashioned was created just before The Fox briefly reopened in June 2020: an optimistic bright spot of hope in what had already been a very dark year. We were all nervous and a little rusty, frightened of bringing in guests and still enveloped in grief for the loss of our friend, Albree Sexton. Anxious to reclaim a bit of normalcy, our pitches for that menu meeting were strange and esoteric, desperately hoping that if the drinks were interesting enough, people might show up and care.

Obviously, we ended up having to close our doors again, so this drink never saw the light of day. But it remains, like that week, a brief hint of a summer unencumbered. Bright and warm and gone too quickly.

> 1½ ounces Mellow Corn whiskey
>
> ½ ounce Rhum Clement Select Barrel
>
> ½ ounce charred corn stock*
>
> ¼ ounce white miso honey**

All ingredients should be kept chilled, and when ready to serve, pour into the serving glass with a large ice cube and gently stir to incorporate. Garnish with a fresh sage leaf and an expression of lemon oil.

*TO MAKE CHARRED CORN STOCK

3 fresh-shucked corn cobs

Organic coconut oil

3 cups water

Lightly rub 3 cobs of corn with organic coconut oil and grill over high flame until lightly blackened in spots. Cut off the cob and add kernels, the halved cobs, and 4-5 fresh sage leaves to 3 cups of water. Simmer, covered, for 30 minutes.

Remove from heat and allow to rest for 30 minutes before straining through a fine mesh nut milk bag, squeezing firmly to remove all liquids.

**TO MAKE WHITE MISO HONEY

2 tablespoons wildflower honey

1 tablespoon white miso paste

1 tablespoon hot water

Combine all ingredients in a sealed container and shake until the miso is fully dissolved. Refrigerate.

SHERRY
COBBLER
p. 128

LOST, FOUND, AND VERMOUTH ALL AROUND

When I stepped away from working in bars and restaurants after most of them had been shut down in late March 2020, I wasn't sure what I would end up doing with my life, other than becoming a house husband and vacuuming *a lot.* →

Much of my time would be spent with my two children, Henry and Leila, aged four and seven, respectively. As of writing this in March 2021, they are still in school virtually and, with the aid of their gracious grandparents, can often be found jumping on the new trampoline in the backyard, even when the weather is cold and gray. At this point, signs are pointing toward them being back in school by the fall, as vaccinations increase and life as we once knew it begins to morph into whatever the new normal will eventually be.

Many of the events I had on the calendar to promote my first book *Garden to Glass: Grow Your Drinks from the Ground Up* during the spring and summer of 2020, in cities as far-flung as Santa Barbara, Chicago, New York, and Atlanta, involved going to these places and making drinks with what was in season at that time. This was my bread and butter. It was what I wrote about in *Garden to Glass* and something I had a lot of experience doing while running the bar at Husk in Nashville for over five years. Part of the core of my hospitality was sharing many of the herbs, vegetables, and flowers I grew myself, and using them in beverage form. I would bring in vast, diverse bouquets of everything from dill flowers to Queen Anne's lace, from bright orange nasturtium flowers to the exotic purple shiso that thrived in my garden, and use them in cordials, liqueurs, bitters, and aromatic, eye-popping garnishes. As the virus raged through the middle of 2020, and with all the time I suddenly had to put my focus back on the garden itself, I felt a certain emptiness since I wouldn't be sharing the bounty of my garden with the guests at my bar. What was I to do with all this wild purple shiso taking over the garden when most of the restaurants I'd either be going to or working in were closed? Enter a lifelong dream to make an ingredient that is a cornerstone of the cocktail: Vermouth.

As I used to love to do with guests, let me tell you the truth about vermouth: it makes life more enjoyable by being delicious, aromatic, quite possibly (but not, you know, legally) medicinal, and crucial to two of life's great pleasures, the martini and the Manhattan. We happen to be entering the golden age of vermouth in America. Maybe even the golden age of vermouth period. As I've spent the last several months researching, tasting, and testing, I've found that a few of my absolute favorite vermouths came not from the capitol of vermouth, Turin, Italy, but from the goddamn, put-your-hands-on-your-belt-buckle United States of America. As we look to emerge from quarantine and this period of heavy drinking, during which the *Miami Herald* reported that alcohol consumption increased by 27 percent overall and by as much as 243 percent in the first few weeks of lockdowns in late March, it could be time to look to more low ABV spirits. With a little more alcohol than wine but less than half the amount of your typical vodka, vermouth-forward drinks are an elegant contrast to the stiff drinks of 2020. I wanted to try my hand at making a vermouth that spoke to the bounty of a garden in late summer, with wormwood flowering alongside lush basil plants and shiso, as mint blossomed and the dill grew as tall as four feet high. I picked what I could and hung it all up to dry.

Botanical alchemy is all well and romantic, but what you really need to make vermouth is good wine. Tyler Alkins, founder of Love and Exile Wines, and I have been talking about making vermouth for a few years now. With his operation on Main Street in East Nashville, minutes from downtown, nearly destroyed in the tornado of March 2020, Tyler spent most of 2020 rebuilding the main floor of his tasting room and the attached restaurant and bar space, where the roof was ripped off. Late last summer, as we looked toward a dark winter and more lockdowns, the time seemed right to begin steeping ingredients and experimenting with a long-term project.

The garden was in full bloom. Shiso was fragrant and flowering, and the Tennessee mountain mint I had been growing for the past five years had taken up a four by six foot corner of the garden, playing host to a cacophony of pollinators. Lemon balm, twinkling with white flowers and the sheen of the herb's oil on the green leaves, was in shorter supply since it was the only green thing I could get the kids to eat lately.

I began harvesting herbs, cutting plenty of lemon verbena, flowering wormwood with its signature bitter bite, and yarrow to hang up to dry. I cut six large bushels of shiso to hang up to dry and noticed as the days unfolded and the herbs dried in the stairway that the shiso took on more of a "hard spice" aroma, smelling like clove and cinnamon wrapped in basil. I decided I would complement those emerging flavors and ordered some Ceylon cinnamon and clove.

By the time I had foraged, harvested, and ordered other ingredients, I had a crazy list of botanicals. To begin, we steeped the dried herbs in seventy gallons of Love and Exile's dry rosé, a garnache from Spain, one of my favorite things that Tyler makes. After a month, I added the hard spices, along with some vanilla beans and juniper berries. Two weeks later, we fortified the wine with a neutral grain spirit and took out the hard spices, which were slowly taking over the herbs, and added some robust botanicals to broaden the flavor profile. This is when some of the backbone vermouth ingredients were added: dandelion root, angelica, gentian root, and dried chrysanthemum flowers. A few months later, I added a honey syrup and cara cara orange zest to open up the flavor and mitigate some of the snappy bitterness that was taking hold. Considering that the whole project could have gone completely wrong—I was concerned about wasting a ton of wine if the flavor went south—we were very happy with the complexity and pleasant dry character of the vermouth.

One of the things I love about vermouth is its versatility. It can be the star ingredient in a low octane cocktail, or it can play the supporting role in a luscious, complex drink. Vermouth goes well with summer berries, fresh herbs, citrus, and champagne, and it can be friendly with almost any spirit. As of now, we've got plans to make more vermouth and host some classes about the history of the category and the diverse styles and regions of this fortified wine. I'd like to share a few things about vermouth that could be of use to the home bartender:

+ Always store your vermouth in the refrigerator and keep the cap tightly closed to limit the amount of oxygen getting into the bottle.

+ When you first open a bottle, note the bouquet and depth of flavor. Then notice how it changes over the course of the first five days it is open.

+ Pour vermouth liberally, and notice how drinking a small amount on its own before a meal makes you salivate in anticipation of food. This was one of its main uses in centuries-old "medicine," to stimulate the appetite.

+ Try to use your bottle of vermouth in the first few weeks after opening it. You'll notice the flavor will flatten out a little if you get to the one-month mark of the bottle being open. One way to use the rest of the vermouth if it's been open too long is to deglaze your pan with it when making a sauce or sautéing meat or vegetables. Simply add some vermouth to the pan while it's hot and scrape up the bits stuck to the pan with a wooden spoon. It will bring a lot of complexity to anything you cook with it.

+ When making cocktails with vermouth, try a little salt or saline solution in the drink. Whether the vermouth is sweet or dry, a tiny amount of salt to go with it will give the drink some umami, making it even more delicious.

As for me, I'm making a resolution to be more like vermouth: open to anything, versatile with whatever is thrown at me, bound to nature, light on my feet, and grateful to be part of a grand tradition.

A NURSE MASTERS THE MARTINI

BY KATE WOLF

Some people have a calling. I am not one of those people. Don't get me wrong—I love what I do, but I can honestly say I went into nursing school because at the time it seemed like my best option. →

Several of my family members had jobs in the medical fiel, and there was a nursing shortage. I like helping people so probably a good fit, right? Aside from the fact that I'm deathly afraid of needles and have been known to pass out from the sight of them, I do enjoy Quentin Tarantino movies. Blood doesn't seem to be a problem, so nursing school it is. While in school, when I realized most of my fellow students had actually worked in a hospital, I quickly decided I should get a job in one. Turns out the only thing that was available for me at the time was in a local emergency room at a level one trauma center. To say it was an eye-opener would be putting it lightly. I learned so many things that I absolutely never would have heard about in school. It was real-world shit and I liked it.

When I finally got my nursing license, it was emergency room all the way for me. This was my place. Despite many of my professors urging me to start in a different field, I felt ready to go straight into the thick of it. I started on night shift, as most new grads do, and came to love the comraderie most of all. At the end of a long, tiring twelve-hour shift, we would often head across the street to a dive bar called the Club 404 for solace. At around 7:15 a.m., we would gather at the back door, which would quickly open like we were VIP at a private show that only *we* knew about, and as we took our seats, the bartender would place a pitcher of Pabst and another of orange juice on the table. "Pabstmosas" is what we called them, and though not a particularly groundbreaking combo, we happily poured them into our glasses. Reminiscing about the night, you would soon hear laughter and pats on the back for a job well done. After moving across the country to Nashville, I learned pretty quickly that this is something universal throughout the industry. Getting off from a night shift and going for a drink with your coworkers is actually very therapeutic. I've had my fair share of beers in the shower when I get home from a hard night, but nothing can replace sharing in the mutual experience of life's harsh realities over a drink at a local dive.

I have now been an emergency room nurse for fifteen years, and when I tell people I work in the ER the question I most often get is: What is the craziest thing you have seen? My answer has now changed. I never would have thought I would experience a pandemic in my nursing career—or lifetime for that matter. It's something you've seen in movies, right? But wouldn't actually happen, would it? Guess again. . . In the beginning, I was mostly in disbelief and denial. This isn't coming here, right!?! It wasn't until a doctor I worked with looked me in the eye in early February of 2020 and said, "It's not a matter of if, but when" that it hit me. We started having to wear masks for our entire shifts and suddenly even touching patients seemed scary. The anxiety came on quickly, and I knew I had to face it and fast. I couldn't be anxious around my patients. My whole job and reason for doing what I do was to help them. I wanted to help them feel at ease. I wanted to help them get through this, and here I was scared to even touch them. In the emergency room I am often meeting people on the worst day of their life, and when that's part of your job, being a source of comfort is one of your biggest goals.

I came to miss those mornings or nights when my colleagues and I could gather over a beer and talk. Laughing over a "Pabstmosa" became a very distant memory. Luckily for me, I had mastered the martini. My husband, Mike, had become quite the mixologist over the years and I became spoiled. I can remember a night (pre-pandemic) when he was working at Chopper and I craved a martini. I was so used to him making them for me that I had never attempted to make one myself. I texted him asking when he would be getting off because I wanted a martini so badly, but he replied it would be late. He then texted me his directions on how to make the ideal martini, but I quickly dismissed it and replied I would wait. I learn best visually, and to my surprise, he decided to teach me when returning home that night. After watching his technique, I was determined to master it. I can now say that he asks me to be the one to make us martinis now. He even asks about my technique . . . shhh . . . it's a secret! When the pandemic began and the bars had to close, my mastery of the martini certainly became handy, although nothing could really replace those social interactions that so many of us longed for. It seemed so ironic to me that when the lockdown started,

I was the only one leaving the house and interacting with others. Mike was always the outgoing one, the one making others laugh when they'd had a bad day. Now it was up to me to learn something else from a master. For the first time, patients were alone except for the healthcare workers around them. Visitors weren't allowed, so we had to step up to be the sole source of comfort to others in an incredibly hard and scary time. A time when our sources of comfort had narrowed. At the end of the day, brightening someone else's day, being a comfort, that is something that I know bartenders have a gift for, and although I am thankful to have mastered the martini, I'd like to think I have mastered far more. Putting people at ease in stressful times and making them feel less alone is one of my strengths, and I've only gotten better at it. I learned from the best. I also make an incredible Old-fashioned now . . . I'll tell you my secret over a martini.

ACKNOWLEDGMENTS

I sincerely want to thank all the amazing contributors to this book for sharing their feelings and insight during a historic time we won't soon forget. There are so many people I've looked up to and enjoyed working with in this book, it's a blessing to have them along for the ride. Thanks to Todd, Ezra, Stephanie, Angie, Heather, Kathleen, Lauren, and everyone at Turner for their support and invaluable assistance with this project. To Brooke Dainty, who did the amazing photography: Thanks so much for crushing it and working so efficiently and with so much care! I really enjoyed our afternoon of furiously whipping up cocktails and setting up drinking scenes all over my house. You are a gem. Thanks to Jess Machen for her beautiful cover, artwork and generous soul. I'm fortunate to work with you, Jess, but we miss you in Nashville!

Thanks so much to Kaitlin Ciarmiello, Andrew Clark, and Ezra Fitz for their incredible insight in editing this book. And of course to my dad, Mark Wolf, the ultimate editor who helped so much when I was lost. To my mom, Cheryl, I know you have been through so much over the last year, and I can't wait to hug you again soon. We'll sit in the backyard with the trees swaying gently while we sip on gin and tonics. I can taste it.

Thanks a million to all the amazing folks with Tennessee Action for Hospitality, like Marcia Masulla and Diana Barton, who have helped so many people in need. You all are an inspiration, and I appreciate you stepping up in the name of hospitality. Thanks to Charlie Nelson, of Nelson's Green Brier Distillery, for making great whiskey and contributing to the cause as well. Thanks a ton to Margaret Littman—a great writer who also wrote a book during a pandemic—for helping to get the word out about the eBook in the *Nashville Scene*. Thanks to everyone at the *Scene* as well, for giving us Nashvillians plenty of perspective over the years.

I have so much respect and admiration for the nurses, doctors, grocery store workers, and other frontline workers who went to work to keep us all afloat during these wild times. Thanks especially to my wife, Kate, who not only wrote a touching afterword to the book, but is an incredible emergency-room nurse and is all our family's hero every day. We are so proud of you, babe; you are a rock star who never loses your sense of humor, and your ethical and moral compass remains as impressive as ever. I admire you so much and love you more with every passing day.

To my kids, Henry and Leila, I am so impressed with the way you have handled this difficult year. Leila, you are a shining light in our family and a constant source of inspiration and hope to me. You went from being uncomfortable with the challenges of virtual school to achieving so much and becoming the best reader in your class. Your creativity and ability to look on the bright side of life will serve you well. You love your family fiercely, and we are all so lucky to have you in our lives. I will always cherish the extra time we had together these last few years. Henry, you are the most fun and hilarious boy we know. You bring us so much joy and laughter, it's a wonder what we ever did without you! I know it was hard for your outgoing personality to be away from so many of your friends and family for so long, but I will always be thankful for the hours on the swings, the times I got you to nap with me on the couch, and all the bedtime stories we read over and over again. Your love of Guns N' Roses at such a young age means we must be doing something right. I'm so grateful for all the time I got to spend with you.

To Cathy and Don Barnett, thanks for being amazing grandparents to our children and for always being there for us. We enjoyed exploring the Tennessee hills with you! I also have to thank everyone at Husk and Josephine. To Chef Andy Little and his wife, Karen, the family atmosphere you have cultivated at Josephine is a beautiful thing, and I'm proud to have been a part of it over the years. To Rory, Katie, Amie, Adam, Kenneth, and everyone else at Husk, thanks for all the support over the years, I love you guys. Thanks also to my brother Matt, Lisa and Anabelle,

Christine and Rob (we miss you dearly), Bob and Ashley Souder, Sean Brock, Brian Baxter, Nate Leonard, Chris, Tracy and Winston of White Squirrel Farms, Kate Tucker and everyone at Garden and Health, Don and Jackie and the family at Simply Living Life, John and Kali Souder and family, Stephen Polcz, Tyler at Love and Exile Wines, Frank Pryor, Matt Campbell, Wilder, Kevin King, Kenny Lyons, Scott Witherow, Kylee at Boothill Kitchen, Tom Maddox, my neighbors Jeremy, Marilyn, Allison, and Siobhan, Sherri, Whit, Cassie, Dale, Dana and the Delworths (not a bad band name, eh?), Marianne and Dave; we are so blessed to have amazing neighbors. Thanks to Larry David, who always makes me laugh so hard, even in the darkest of days. Thanks to you, dear reader.

ABOUT THE AUTHOR

Mike Wolf lives in Nashville, Tennessee with his wife Kathryn, their two children, Henry and Leila, two dogs, June and George, and a wily cat named Boone. He plays and writes music and spends a lot of time outdoors gardening and hiking. Wolf is a beverage industry veteran who hosts the beverage podcast *Liquid Gold*. He opened and established the bar program at Husk Nashville before co-founding the robot tiki haven, Chopper. He is currently making vermouth and working on his first novel. *Cheer: A Liquid Gold Holiday Drinking Guide*, his new book with co-author Kenneth Dedmon, is forthcoming from Turner Publishing.